双城记

威斯敏斯特大学建筑与城市学院
中国中央美术学院建筑学院
国际联合工作室　2015-2020

SERIES INTRODUCTION

Studio as Book is a new series of publications that tender, in detail, the extraordinary creative work undertaken in the design studios at the School of Architecture + Cities. The series includes undergraduate and graduate level work, and is intended to sit alongside the Open Exhibition and catalogue. Each book in the series covers the work of a single design studio over the course of at least two years. Its objectives are:

• To record, archive, and present the pedagogical programme and creative student outputs of a design studio
• To position the work of a design studio within a broader intellectual, scientific or aesthetic field
• To advance the design driven research being undertaken in the School's design studios
• To provide a reference for future iterations and variations of a design studio

Reducing the creative output of a multi-year design studio to a single volume, using a pre-designed book template is no easy undertaking, and it is necessarily selective. At the same time, it provides a consistent, sure platform for the wide range of approaches to the discipline of teaching architectural design which characterise the department.

Each Studio as Book has been peer-reviewed on the basis of a proposal submitted by the studio's tutors to an editorial committee. In addition to studio briefs and student work, each book includes content that draws out the studio's research and pedagogical agenda. The format that this takes varies from book to book – reflective essays by tutors or past students, interviews, theoretical essays from parallel fields, and so forth. The Studio as Book Series will later be accompanied by a Studio Pamphlet Series for design studios of a shorter duration.

I wish to acknowledge the contribution of the following in bringing this project to fruition: Lindsay Bremner, Director of Research, who was the driving force behind the series, Mark Boyce, author of Sizes May Vary, A workbook for graphic design (Lawrence King, 2008) – and the designer of Studio as Book, and Filip Visnjic, designer of the series' web site, http://www.studioasbook.org.

Harry Charrington
Head of School of Architecture + Cities
University of Westminster

FOREWORD

HARRY CHARRINGTON

The Joint International Design (JID) Studio Programme, created by the School of Architecture and Cities at the University of Westminster (A+C) and the School of Architecture at the Central Academy of Fine Arts in China (CAFA), is a testament to the value of project-based partnerships. Led by Dr John Zhang from A+C, Professor Keren He from CAFA, with Professor David Porter working across both institutions, the JID Studio Programme has established itself as a uniquely innovative approach to international exchange and cross-cultural pedagogies. Drawing on their various experiences, the conversations in this book reveal the complementarity of the three tutors; Keren's experience in the China and US education systems, David's extensive practice and educational leadership in the UK, Europe and China, and John's historical and critical knowledge of practice in China and the UK. The diverse multi-culturalism of the students adds another critical layer - this is a Beijing-London exchange more than a British-Chinese one.

From the outset we were determined the exchange would bring something new to each school. For CAFA, this is A+Cs studio culture of a playful experimentation grounded in agreed learning outcomes (to quote Alvar Aalto, "our goals may be rational, but how we get there may not be"), which is very different to the US-tradition of the 'top-down' studio masterclass familiar throughout much of China. For A+C, it is CAFA's status as an art academy offering architecture students constant exposure to a variety of artistic representations which encourage them to push the boundaries of their work beyond conventional techniques. The extensive use of digital technologies has enabled a virtual studio to complement the physical exchanges - more than prescient given the COVID-19 pandemic.

Centred on the poetics of habitat and the art of inhabitation, the JID Studio, nonetheless, did not set out to be a housing studio. Rather, this emerged through its systematic mapping of neighbourhoods in the two cities, and the collation of an informal history of Beijing and London's ever-evolving patterns of urban life. And, while the JID Studio is firmly contemporary in its immediate concerns with taxonomies of housing, it is unbound from the normative formal anxieties of modernism. Instead, grounded in a comparative and re-evaluation of their architectural history and application, its concern is with typicality of use rather than typology, an approach that embodies what David calls 'theory as explanation'.

It is therefore no surprise that the legacy of Neave Brown (whom some students were fortunate enough to visit) and 'Cook's Camden' (discussed here by Douglas Murphy) are apparent in the manner in which the JID Studio addresses the enclaves and exclaves of contemporary urban reality. Underscored by what John Edwards identifies as the urbanity of a 'low-rise high-density tectonic', the JID Studio explores a slippage of types as they inflect to the vagaries and precisions of their site. Courtyard and mat housing gain what John Zhang calls 'informal encrustations and additions' from an intimate and comparative knowledge of each city's building stock, together with contemporary programmes such as the new forms of collectivism that are emerging in the aftermath of the nuclear family. Students remake the familiar, such as the street-facing UK terrace and the Shikumen of Shanghai alleyways, revive lesser-known types such as the shared-entrance Georgian terrace, and assign new kinds of activity to the in-between space of the Hutong street and Siheyuan courtyard.

This temporal grip on what we might call 'urban domesticity' - changing urban morphologies and housing types - is addressed through the JID Studio's commitment to a design practice characterised by Keren's citing of Tao Qin and the ideal of *Yijing* as 'an optimistic imagination for the future'. Determinedly architectural and three-dimensional, the student schemes evoke a sense of the archaeology of their sites and renewed spatial possibilities, as with Signe Pelne's convivial remaking of Fu Guo Li estate. A number of projects deal with London point-block and Beijing lamellar-block estates and their characteristic collision between the claustrophobia of wholly private interiors and the agoraphobia of their amorphously public sites. In these projects, the bases of the blocks are reformulated as a navigable and differentiated urban realm, a city floor of communal living spaces that restores the middle-ground of the neighbourhood.

Over 5-years, the JID Studio staff and students have undertaken a series of precisely located and engaged design projects that have cumulatively built up into the body of knowledge this book showcases. I look forward to the next five years, and hope others will follow its innovative approach and create an equally transformative and global student experience.

CONTENTS

FOREWORD — 004
Harry Charrington

STUDIO INTRODUCTION — 008
John Zhang

ON HOW WE STARTED — 012
Keren He, David Porter, John Zhang

COURTYARDS — 018
John Zhang

Tapestry of Encounter	Signe Pelne
Life Between Buildings	Remi Kuforiji
Hutong Re-imagined	Ryan Myers
Colllectively Detached	Poonam Ale
Learning Landscape	Maheer Khan
Living in the Landscape	Yana Stoyanova
Open Siheyuan	Drew Yates
Garden of Micro-living	Zixiao Tong
Foley for a Living Landscape	Ryan Myers
A New Hutong Archaeology	Signe Pelne

ON HOUSING — 064
Keren He, David Porter, John Zhang

HOUSING IN SECTION — 070
Douglas Murphy

TERRACES — 078
John Zhang

Terrace Re-imagined	Ryan Speer
Mews Meets Landscape	Catalina Stroe
Care in the Community	Lauren Fashokun
Migrants Welcome	Catalina Stroe
Growing Old Together	Gabija Gumbevileciute
Crossing Strata	Anna Tabacu
Scholars' Garden	Poonam Ale
Half Way House	Drew Yates
Up Market	Matt Lindsay
Shikumen in London	Lucy Bambury

ON ENCLAVES AND THRESHOLDS — 118
Keren He, David Porter, John Zhang

EAST MEETS WEST — 126
John Zhang

LINEAR BLOCKS 136
John Zhang

Art of Living	Rebecca Cooper
Framing Beijing	Pengfei Gao
Old and Young	Hugo Shackleton
Vertical Co-Housing	Aristides Jones
Lives of Artists	Bryan Espinoza
Vertical Kink	Zeyuan Shi
Landscape Therapy	Irina Bodrova
Nature-Hood	Karol Wozniak
Up the Wall	Yufan Xie
A Monument of Minimal Living	Matt Lindsay

ON A COMPARATIVE PEDAGOGY 182
Keren He, David Porter, John Zhang

A MOMENT IN BEIJING 194
Signe Pelne

PERIMETER BLOCKS 198
John Zhang

24 Hour Block	Anissa Colaco De Souza
Re-Habitation	Jasmine Montina
Open Campus	Gia San Tu
Happy Together	Barbara Cellario
Panoramic Refuge	Jacqueline Rosales
Courtyards in the Sky	Remi Kuforiji
Meet Your Neighbours	Rebecca Cooper
Resilient Refuge	Kristina Veleva
Variations on a Quad	Billy Nguyen
A New Urban Village	Ryan Speer

ON THE POETICS OF HABITAT 242
Keren He, David Porter, John Zhang

A CONVERSATION OF RELEVANCE 246
John Edwards

AFTERTHOUGHT: NOSTALGIA, SENTIMENTALITY AND THE NEED TO TRAVEL 250
John Zhang

LEARNING FROM BEIJING: A VISUAL ESSAY 254

ACKNOWLEDGEMENTS 302

STUDIO INTRODUCTION

JOHN ZHANG

As architects and educators, we cannot ignore the fact that globalisation and communication technologies have had a homogenising effect on our built environment. Yet, simultaneously, the focus on identity politics, regional culture and traditions have made our opinions more polarised than before. In navigating these contradictions and complexities, the conventional, static, isolated architectural education model has to adopt a more dynamic, inter-disciplinary, cross-cultural and collaborative approach.

This is precisely what the Joint International Design (JID) Studio, was established to do. We are an experimental 3rd year undergraduate design studio, based at the University of Westminster, and taught in conjunction with the Central Academy of Fine Arts (CAFA) in China. Using Beijing and London as our testbeds, we advocate an architecture that engages the global context and explore new ideas of living together in the global city.

Our studio is built around an extensive annual programme of exchanges between the two institutions. It allows the students to see first hand how architecture is made and experienced in a radically different urban and cultural context, where they visit some ancient monuments, as well as some of the most innovative new buildings in the world. We encourage students to think comparatively about the radically different urban morphologies of London and Beijing, to undercover the nuances of their similarities and differences, and gain insights into what makes them successful and what challenges they both face. We constantly question what it takes to think in context, posed as a general problem in human thought and as a particular problem for architects.

These fundamental concerns and curiosities form the basis for a pair of housing design projects undertaken by the students over the course of each academic year, sited in Beijing and London respectively. The ubiquity and universality of housing as a basic tenet of human life and a fundamental constituent of our cities, provide us with a common ground and a point of departure for developing new concepts and novel tectonics, to learn from each other and to look at things afresh. We aim to impress upon the students the reality of how the built environment is commissioned, designed, delivered and critiqued. We engage with local authorities on their roles as clients, invite architects working on our sites to divulge their creative processes, visit the studios of creative practices in Beijing and London, and ask sociologists who are engaged in resident consultation to tell us all they know about our users. We ask established architects, writers and educators to critique our work. We choose sites in Beijing and London that are on the verge of genuine and immanent transformation, where issues of rising property prices, de-industrialisation, gentrification, an ageing population, and mass migration are just some of the shared challenges reshaping our cities. We ask the students to be critically aware of how spatial production takes place within the reality of specific socio-economic and political systems, be it capitalism or Socialism with Chinese Characteristics.

In developing their design proposals, we ask the students to pay close attention to the details of people's spatial idiosyncrasies: how they occupy space at a human scale and mediate the thresholds between public and private, between the inside and the outside, and between the building and the city. For us, research is done through the act of making, be it drawings, models, collages, or films. Ultimately, we seek conceptually innovative and formally novel ideas, drawn from the richness of a global experience, and developed at both the dwelling scale as well as the urban scale.

Included in this book is a collection of student projects that best illustrate this collective endeavour. These visions are informed by our exploration of the typologies that currently shape our cities, where Beijing norms inspire London experiments, and vice versa. As such, the student work is not organised chronologically or geographically, but rather, in the spirit of our comparative and global perspective, organised by type, where courtyards, terraces, perimeter blocks and linear blocks have the potential to inspire original responses in London or Beijing. The projects, at times raw and unresolved, nevertheless contain moments of real insight and originality, of novel tectonics and innovative prototypes, which begin to shed some light on how we might all wish to live in the future.

Of course, our collective endeavour is much more than a compendium of student projects. Critically, the studio is about creating and facilitating conversations, collaborations and contributions. Over the last four years, the studio tutors, the students, our regular collaborators, and our invited critics have been engaged in an ongoing conversation as we developed our comparative pedagogical approach. We have retraced the lineage of east-west engagement in architecture, discussed the histories of housing in London and Beijing, debated cultural nuances in spatial habits and talked over differences in architectural pedagogies. This book includes a collection of these contemplations in the form of conversations and essays from ourselves and our collaborators.

So this is a tale of two cities, but it asks a singular universal question: how can we, through our collective and collaborative endeavours, create a new poetics of habitat.

ON HOW WE STARTED

KEREN HE, DAVID PORTER, JOHN ZHANG

The Joint International Design (JID) Studio was born out of, and continues to evolve through a dialogue between cultures, theories, methods, and most importantly, between people. This is often a 'tria-logue', between Dr John Zhang from the University of Westminster, Professor He Keren from the Central Academy of Fine Arts, and Professor David Porter - visiting professor at both institutions, who have collectively shaped the joint programme.

Keren He (KH) is a Beijinger who has studied architecture at Tsinghua, and then onto the University of Notre Dame in the U.S., where she also worked as an architect in New York. She was the visiting scholar at University of Applied Arts Vienna from 2012 to 2013, and now a PhD candidate studying under her advisor, the architectural historian Liane Lefaivre at University of Applied Arts, Vienna. She has been teaching at CAFA since 2005, where she is now the director of International Programs, Studio Master of CAFA International Exchange Studio and Thesis Studio 16.

David Porter (DP) is a Londoner, who over his long career has worked and taught widely. Having studied at the Bartlett, he joined Neave Brown and worked on some of the most exciting modernist housing projects in London. He later became a partner in Neave Brown David Porter Architects working on high-density urban projects in the Netherlands that were published and exhibited in Europe, the USA and Japan. He was the Head of the Mackintosh School of Architecture at the Glasgow School of Art (2000-11). He founded the Glasgow Urban Laboratory, a partnership between the Mackintosh School of Architecture and Glasgow City Council in 2007 and was elected as an Academician at the Academy of Urbanism. He was Visiting Professor at the Arkitektskolen Aarhus, Denmark. From 2011-14 he was Adjunct Professor in the School of Architecture & Design at the Royal Melbourne Institute of Technology. He was the President of the Architectural Association (2015-8). Between 2012 and 2018 he was Professor of Architecture at the Central Academy of Fine Art, Beijing.

John Zhang (JZ) was born in China, but moved to London when he was 10, and grew up in the UK. After studying at Cambridge then the RCA he was involved in full time practice for many years at design led practice DSDHA, working on projects across a wide range of scales and sectors. His connection to and interest in China eventually led to him into research and teaching, whilst maintaining a small personal studio. He completed a PhD at the RCA between 2013 and 2017, on the relationship between foreign and Chinese architects. At about the same time, he became involved in teaching at the University of

David discussing housing with CAFA students on a visit to Alexander Road Estate

Westminster, running the JID studio from 2015.

From their different perspectives, John, Keren and David have been engaged in a continuous conversation over the last 5 years as they developed the studio's programme, approach and focus. This has been a process of figuring out what the studio is doing by induction, trial and error, what the social sciences might term as a 'Grounded' approach. Critical to this process is the act of a dialectical conversation between the three, where ideas are floated, exchanged, discussed, reflected upon, and absorbed. As such, to tell the story of the studio, one must go back to these conversations.

This is the first of 4 essays that take the form of a conversation, or a 'tria-logue', between John, Keren and David. In this first conversation, the team recalls the history of the JID and how it has come about.

JZ: The JID, or China Studio, as it is often known to the students, started in 2013-2014, but as I understand, the International Exchange Studio at CAFA, which the JID studio joins every year for 8 weeks, was conceived under a pilot programme a year before. Keren, could you tell us a little about its origins? David, how did you become involved?

KH: The idea of setting up an international studio at CAFA School of Architecture was conceived between 2012 and 2013. I was just back from Vienna after completing a year-long visiting scholar program at the University of Applied Arts. Ann-Elisabeth Toft and Claudia Carbone from Aarhus School of Architecture of Denmark came to CAFA and wanted to discuss a joint Masters program with CAFA students. Lü Pinjing, then the Dean of the Architectural School, asked me to be in charge of this. Thus was the beginning of this special studio.

With Ms. Toft and Ms. Carbone from Aarhus, and Wei Wang and I from CAFA, we set up a 5-week urban research program in Beijing participated by over 30 Aarhus and CAFA Masters students in the fall semester of 2012. Then, in 2013, we took 10 students to Aarhus and continued this program in the 'Studio of Constructing an Archive' led by Ms. Toft and Ms. Carbone. It was at this exhibition in Aarhus where we officially came up with the name the International Exchange Studio. In the following fall semester of 2014-15 at CAFA we established a 20-week urban and housing design program that ran parallel to the 4th year undergraduate curriculum, including 6 bachelor students, 10 master students from CAFA, and 5

International and Chinese students discussing models in the CAFA studio

Students taking photos at the Beijing Olympic Park

exchange students from Switzerland, Germany and Austria. David Porter, Siyong Liu, Wei Wang and I were the tutors. Tao Han and Xiaolei Hou later joined the tutor team. The next year we started to incorporate a 4-week program with the University of Westminster of London; a joint effort has been continuing ever since.

DP: I became involved in the exchange studio through a mixture of luck and chance. I had been invited by Dean Lü Pinjing to teach at CAFA starting in the Autumn of 2012. Prof Lü and I had both participated in a network of European architectural educators that would meet regularly to discuss ideas and developments.

Prof Lü asked me to give lectures on architectural theory to the CAFA masters students. I was not keen on lecturing to them – I wanted to interact with them, more like in a studio, so I led seminars rather than giving lectures. And I did not want to import second-hand Western theories into China – I was more interested in my students learning to 'theorise' for themselves. To help me, I teamed me up with Wang Wei, a CAFA graduate who had subsequently studied at Delft.

As a foreigner, I was learning from Beijing: exploring, scratching my head and asking myself: "what?"; "why?"; "how?". I was learning from Beijing. We asked our students to investigate the qualities of a series of buildings in Beijing, old and new, exploring the buildings as phenomena rather than as historical relics or contemporary manifestos. We asked them to investigate these places as designers, learning to appreciate them as designed artefacts, and so seeing Beijing with fresh eyes. Their reports on these places and the descriptions they gave, were an act of theorising: the articulate interaction between words, sketches, diagrams, photographs, and videos. Then we found ways to discuss and compare the results – to 'theorise them'. Theorising the places and theorising the means we used to represent them.

For me 'theory' is really a grand word for 'explanation'. I was teaching an approach to designing and to design research that is based on close observation and experiment, rather than on the imposition of theory. This approach was what in Western philosophy would be called 'empiricism'.

I had just started these 'theorising' seminars when I bumped into another member of the European network

The studio on a visit to the Hutongs of Beijing

of architectural educators, Ann-Elizabeth Toft from the architecture school in Aarhus in Denmark. Her involvement with CAFA was a happy surprise. She had brought a group of Danish students to collaborate with a CAFA group led by Keren He. So, I met Keren through Ann-Elizabeth.

My seminars involved an observational approach which encompassed exploring and explaining spatial relationships, in other words, mapping. This was very similar to the approach that Ann-Elizabeth and Keren were adopting in their studio. I invited Ann-Elizabeth to join my seminars and contribute, which she did, and at Keren's invitation, I gave some of my master's presentations to the students of the CAFA-Aarhus collaborative studio. All of this was unplanned – it just happened, and it seemed to work well. These collaborations were the precursors of what grew into the 'China Studio'.

At the same time, something else was emerging that contributed to the future exchange studio. For the group from Aarhus were not the only foreign exchange students at CAFA. There was another loose group of individual exchange students, from different schools mainly in Northern Europe and Switzerland, who found out that I was running a seminar programme in the evenings in English, and so they began joining me and I asked them to team-up in small groups that mixed cultures. Like the Aarhus-CAFA studio this unplanned mix of Chinese and European students also contributed to the formation of the Exchange Studio.

JZ: Yes, this was the point at which students from Westminster became part of the story. At that time, I was moving from being a full-time practitioner into academia, becoming involved in teaching studio at Westminster and finishing a PhD at the Royal College of Art on the relationship between Chinese and foreign architects. I had wanted to explore China in a studio teaching context for some time. It was around then that Harry Charrington, our Head of School, who had visited Beijing, got in touch with me and asked if I wanted to teach on a small but experimental studio in collaboration with CAFA.

So, it was the fortuitous coming together of us all that ended up in the creation of the JID Studio, as it is known at Westminster. The first cohort of 6 UK students arrived in Beijing in the autumn of 2013 and stayed at CAFA four weeks.
In the following years, the studio has grown to around 10 students every year, studying in CAFA for two months. The students from Westminster now make up a third of the CAFA International Exchange Studio for the duration of their stay in Beijing and have become an integral part of the programme. It has been fascinating to see the evolution of the studio, which in my opinion has grown organically, shaped by the confluence and convergence of students and tutors from all over the world. The Grounded approach of the studio reminds me of a Chinese saying: 'wading the river by feeling the stones'. That is to say, we are all engaged in a collective journey, in which the only way forward is to learn inductively and learn from each other.

COURTYARDS

JOHN ZHANG

The courtyard, typically arranged as set of interior spaces surrounding an external space open to the sky, is a pattern of spatial organisation widely used across the world. It is an adaptive and flexible response to a variety of climatic, topographical, material, cultural and socio-economic challenges, both historically and contemporaneously.

The courtyard is synonymous with the way traditional architecture and urban pattern are organised in China. At the root of this spatial language is the Siheyuan: a four sided walled residence oriented north to south, with four single-storey rooms, inter-connected by covered walkways, arranged along its cardinal edges, overlooking a central external hard paved courtyard.

This is the basic module of traditional Chinese living, which in repetition, variation and magnification defined the architectures of dwellings, businesses, palaces and temples.

In Beijing, the tight accumulation of Siheyuans, accessed via narrow and meandering alleys known as Hutongs, have historically defined the urban identity of the city. From being the home of a single family, the Beijing Siheyuan has withstood countless re-appropriation and redefinition of its programmatic orders, including informal encrustations and additions, as well as the threat of wholesale demolition. The intrinsic tectonic qualities of the Siheyuan has allowed it to adapt to different forms of occupation, and to not only survive but maintain its value and relevance to the city.

Looking at the Siheyuan typology from a western perspective, the urbanism it creates is radically different from its European counterpart, particularly concerning the relationship between dwellings and the street, where the principal façades face inwards to the internal courtyard, and the home turns its back on the Hutong alley outside, which remains a labyrinth of mystery for anyone who does not belong to the immediate community. However, this does not mean that there is no dialogue to be had between East and West. At the fundamental level, the Siheyuan and the urbanism it creates can be described as belonging to a mat typology: typically understood as a low rise tectonic strategy of alternating and inter-connected interior and exterior spaces, based on the repetition and variation of a fundamental 'unit' or 'module'.

The mat building type has been a periodically recurrent preoccupation of architects within the western architectural discourse, particularly since the onset of modernism. Le Corbusier's Venice Hospital plans and the designs of the Free University of Berlin by Candilis, Josic, Woods and Schiedhelm are often referenced as seminal examples of this approach. The term itself was given prominence by the writings of Alison Smithson, who believed that 'Mat-building can be said to epitomise the anonymous collective; where the functions come to enrich the fabric, and the individual gains new freedoms of action through a new and shuffled order, based on interconnection, close-knit patterns of association, and possibilities for growth, diminution, and change.' [01], In more recent decades, the fascination with 'fields' in architectural theories has unleashed a renewed interest in the typology.

Given the explicit nature of the courtyard typology in Beijing and the wide ranging European experimentations with the mat pattern of spatial and urban organisation, it is unsurprising that students from this studio has produced a diverse array of experiments in courtyard living and mat urban patterns. Through their explorations, the students have interrogated how this fundamental typology can be re-imagined to address contemporary issues. Of particular note are Signe Pelne and Ryan Myer, who both tested how the Siheyuan Hutong typology could be re-invented to create higher density, more ambiguous thresholds with the rest of the city, and integrate with nature and landscape, as well as to facilitate communities that live through sharing. Amongst the other students, many explored with augmentations of the traditional four sided courtyard to create more flexible patterns of inhabitation and a better relationship with the landscape.

Notes

(01) Alison Smithson, How to Recognise and Read Mat-Building, *Architectural Design,* September, 1974

TAPESTRY OF ENCOUNTERS

SIGNE PELNE

LOCATION: HOLBORN, LONDON, UK

This proposal seeks to reconnect a neglected post-war era council estate through the creative use of the courtyard typology as an urban mat that restitches the broken neighbourhood with the rest of the city.

Inspired by the Siheyuan courtyard typology in Beijing, a series of inter-connected cloistered garden courtyards reclaim the left over spaces around a pair of poorly planned post-war housing tower blocks. Each courtyard garden is enclosed by a variety of dwelling types, from studios for students to homes for families. The modular nature of the dwelling types creates a range of differently sized shared courtyards, the corners of which contain spaces for shared communal activities, from shared dining rooms to guest bedrooms. The adjacencies of these courtyards to each other and the existing buildings on site create an overlay of the public over the communal.

As one moves from room to room, inside to outside, courtyard to courtyard, a series of programmed and un-programmed spaces are revealed, varying in sizes and proportions, blurring the boundary between the private, the communal, and the public. This ambiguity then become the stages on which existing and new residents are brought together in a tapestry of encounters.

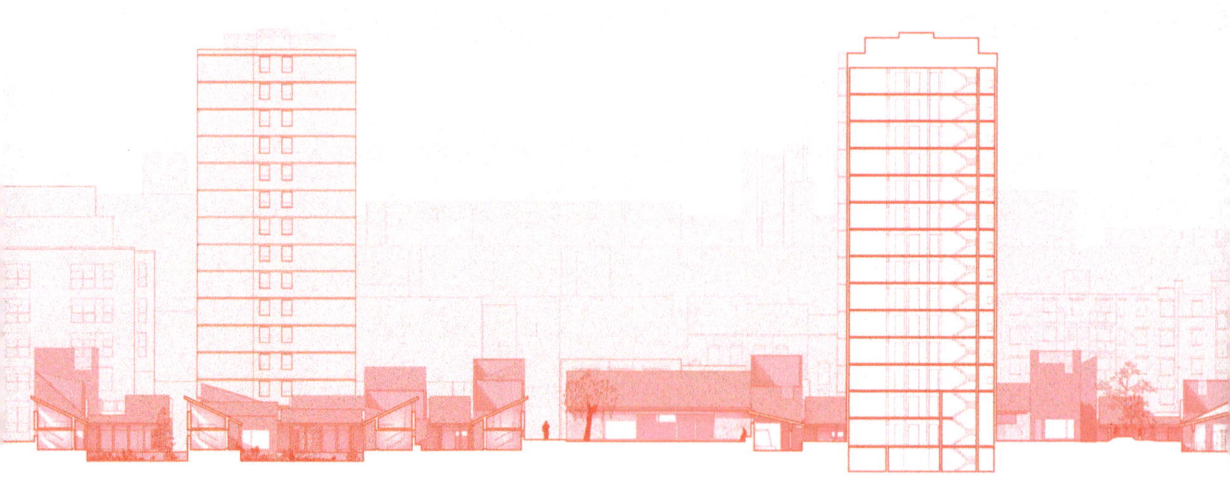

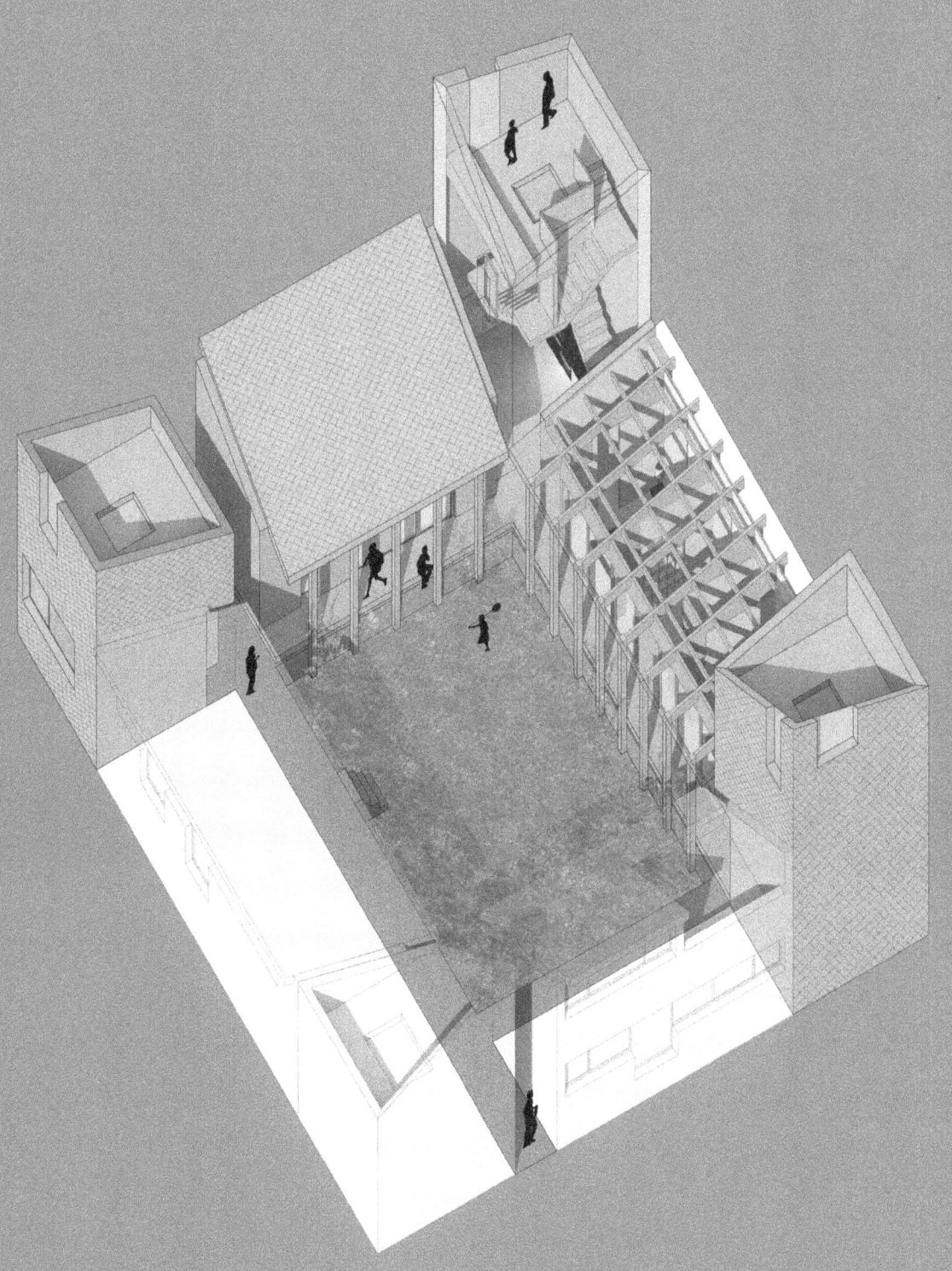

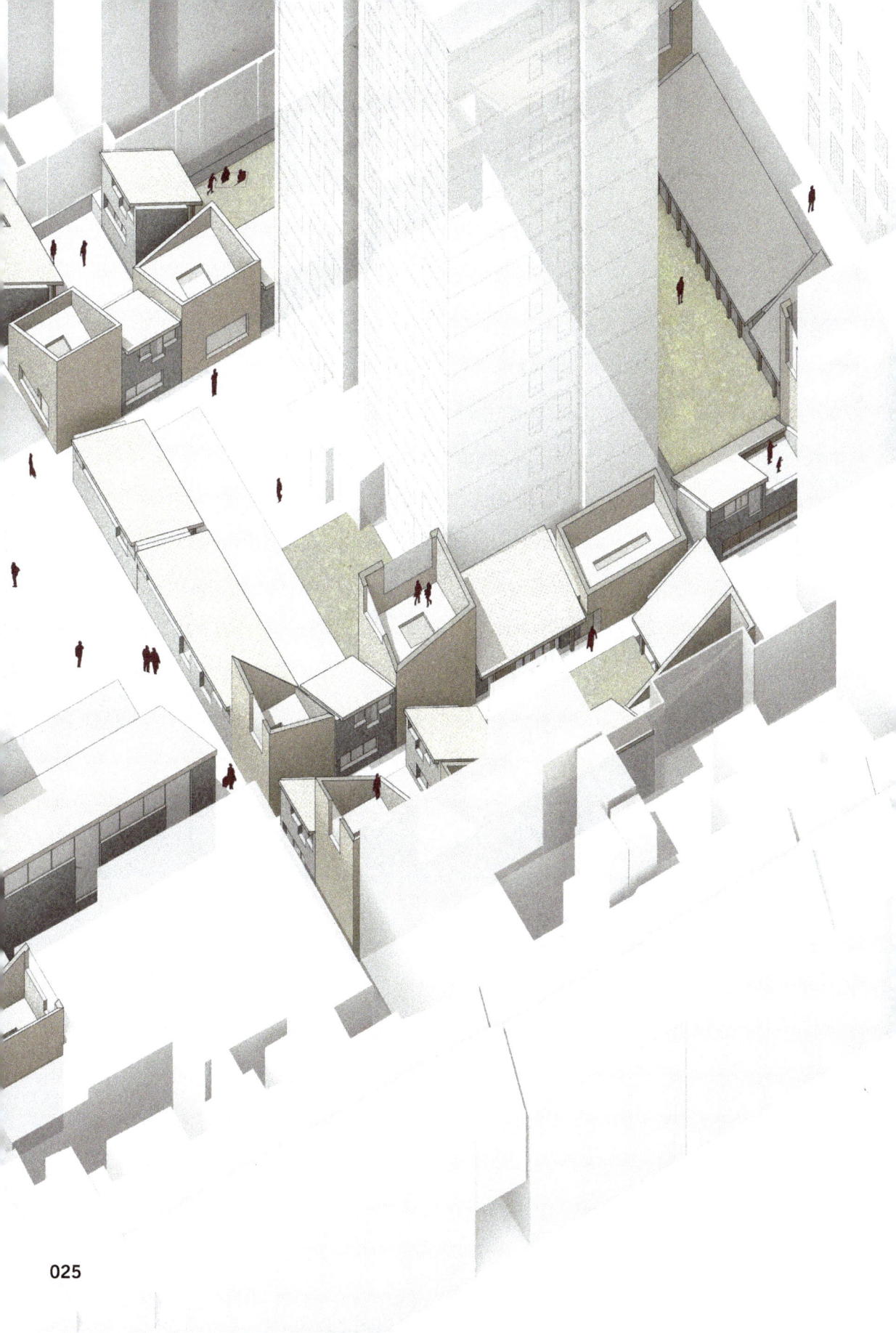

LIFE BETWEEN BUILDINGS

REMI KUFORIJI

LOCATION: HOLBORN, LONDON, UK

This project re-conceptualises the idea of the living room as a fluid and permeable space that changes with time and can be variably shared amongst family, friends, and neighbours.

The conventional relationship between the courtyard form and the ground is inverted by raising the orthogonal enclosure aloft, creating a covered and sheltered ground floor with a double height atrium at its centre. This space becomes a place of shared potentials. Flexible external sliding folding facade and internal partitions allow the entire ground floor to be augmented to suit the residents' specific needs as their circumstances change on a daily basis. Working from a uniform grid imposed over the open plan, and the wider site, temporary dining rooms, guest bedrooms, games rooms, greenhouses come into being and then disappear as part of this flexible communal 'living room', which can also shrink in size and become grounds for public encounters.

When these communal 'living rooms' are brought together as an ensemble that fill the neglected space within a post-war council estate, the cumulative effect is a new kind of public realm, in which the boundary between the private, the communal, and the public becomes ambiguous, where changeable encounters promotes a sense of community.

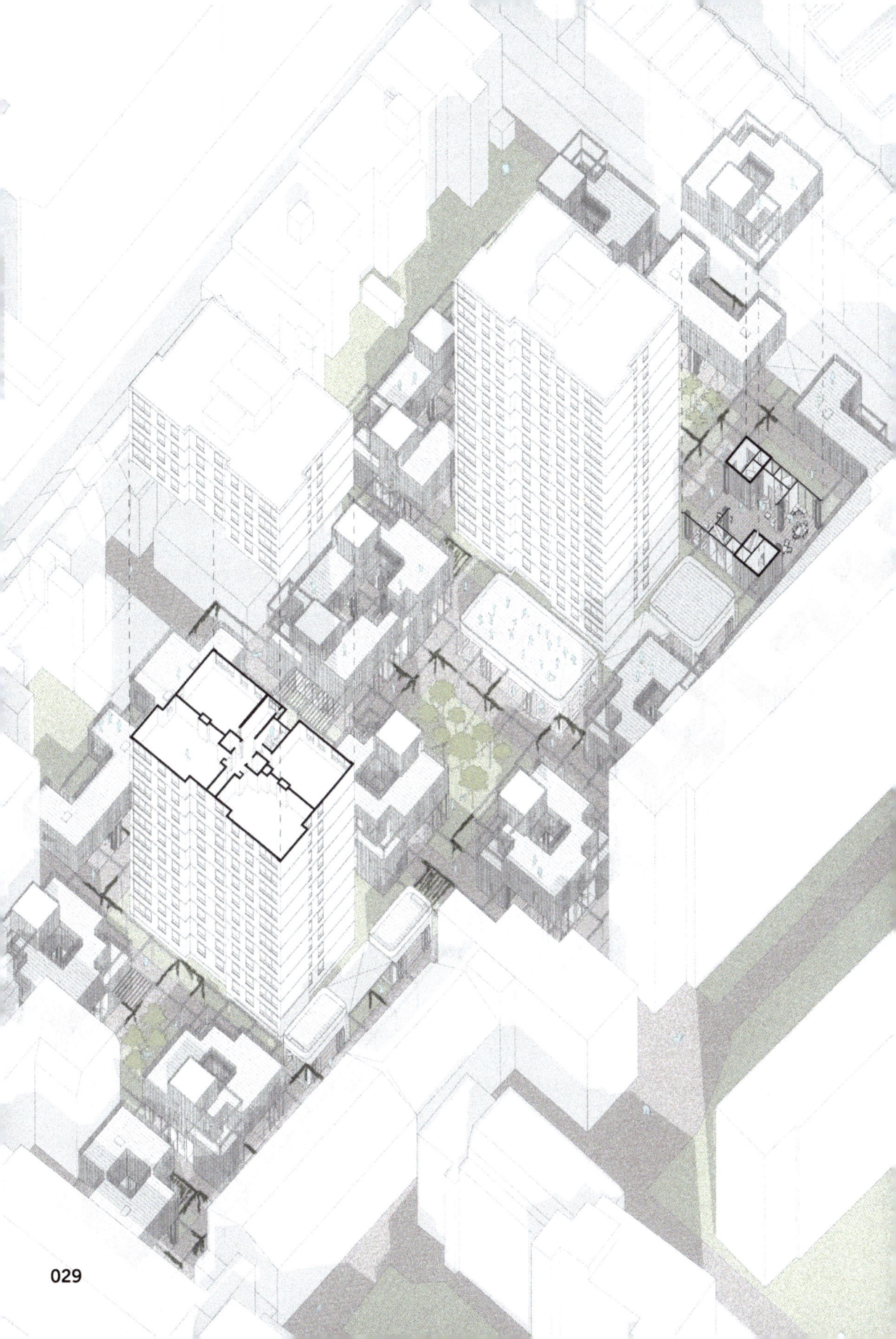

HUTONG RE-IMAGINED

RYAN MAYERS

LOCATION: SAN YUAN LI, BEIJING, CHINA

This project asks if the Siheyuan courtyard typology and the Hutong urban pattern can be re-imagined with greater density, variety and sustainability.

In place of the traditional Siheyuan, which in its origin was only intended for a single extended family, the proposal responds to Beijing's changing demographic constituency and creates a re-imagined Siheyuan made of 5 households over 2 levels, perfect for students, co-habiting friends or young couples. The generosity of the courtyard is preserved as a realm of shared amenity, but the augmented tectonic includes a spare bedroom on the ground floor for visiting friends, lodgers, or grandparents. A common staircase gives access to the two 1st floor apartments and a communal roof terrace. The roof terrace is encased in a structural frame which allows the 1st floor apartments to expand in the future and become family homes, adding extra flexibility to the housing mix. The interior arrangement is inspired by the traditional 'kang' of northern China, where a rammed earth raised bed is connected to and heated by the kitchen stove, a highly sustainable energy strategy.

Tested on an awkward left over triangular site in Beijing, the proposal demonstrates its ability to become an urban connecting mat, creating a new kind of Hutong of intimate cross-crossing alleys and occasional opens spaces serving the community.

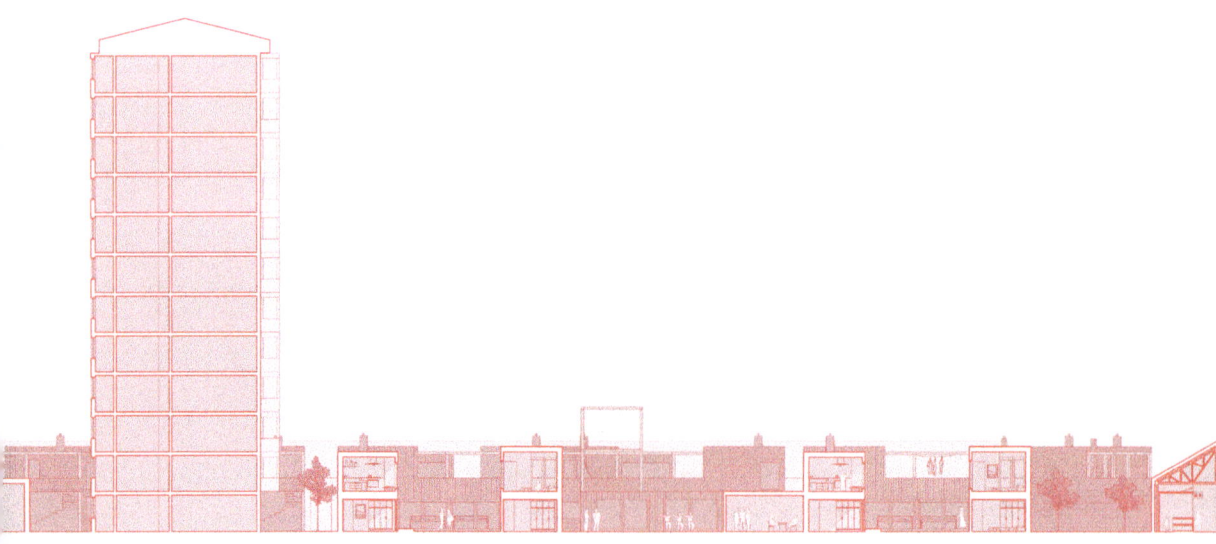

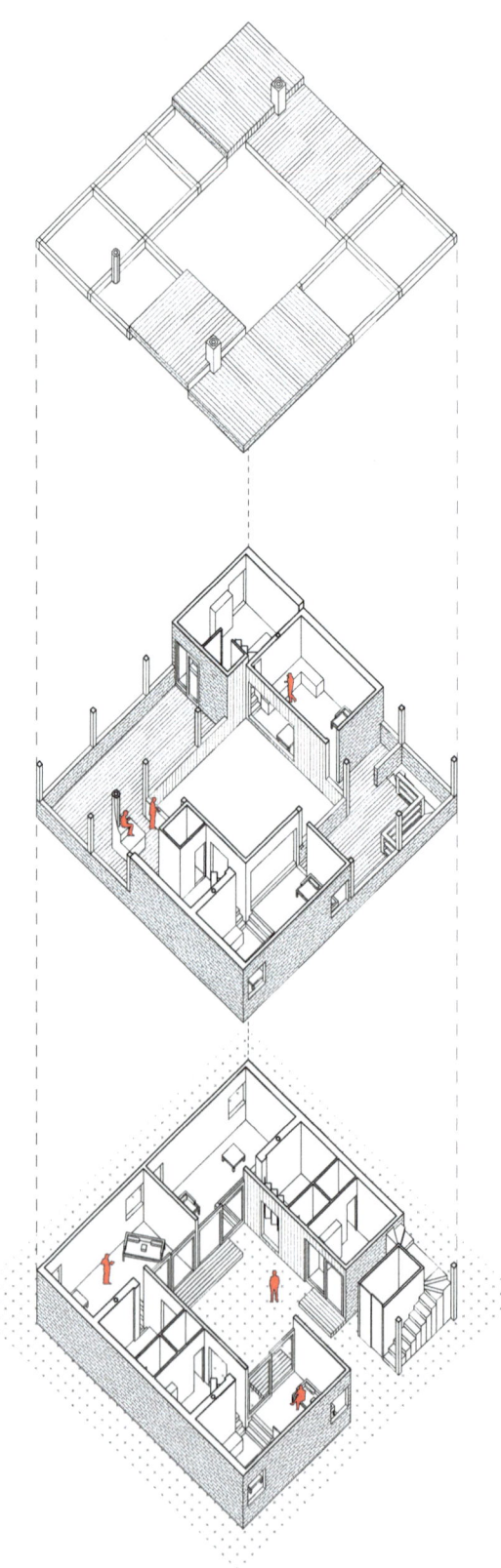

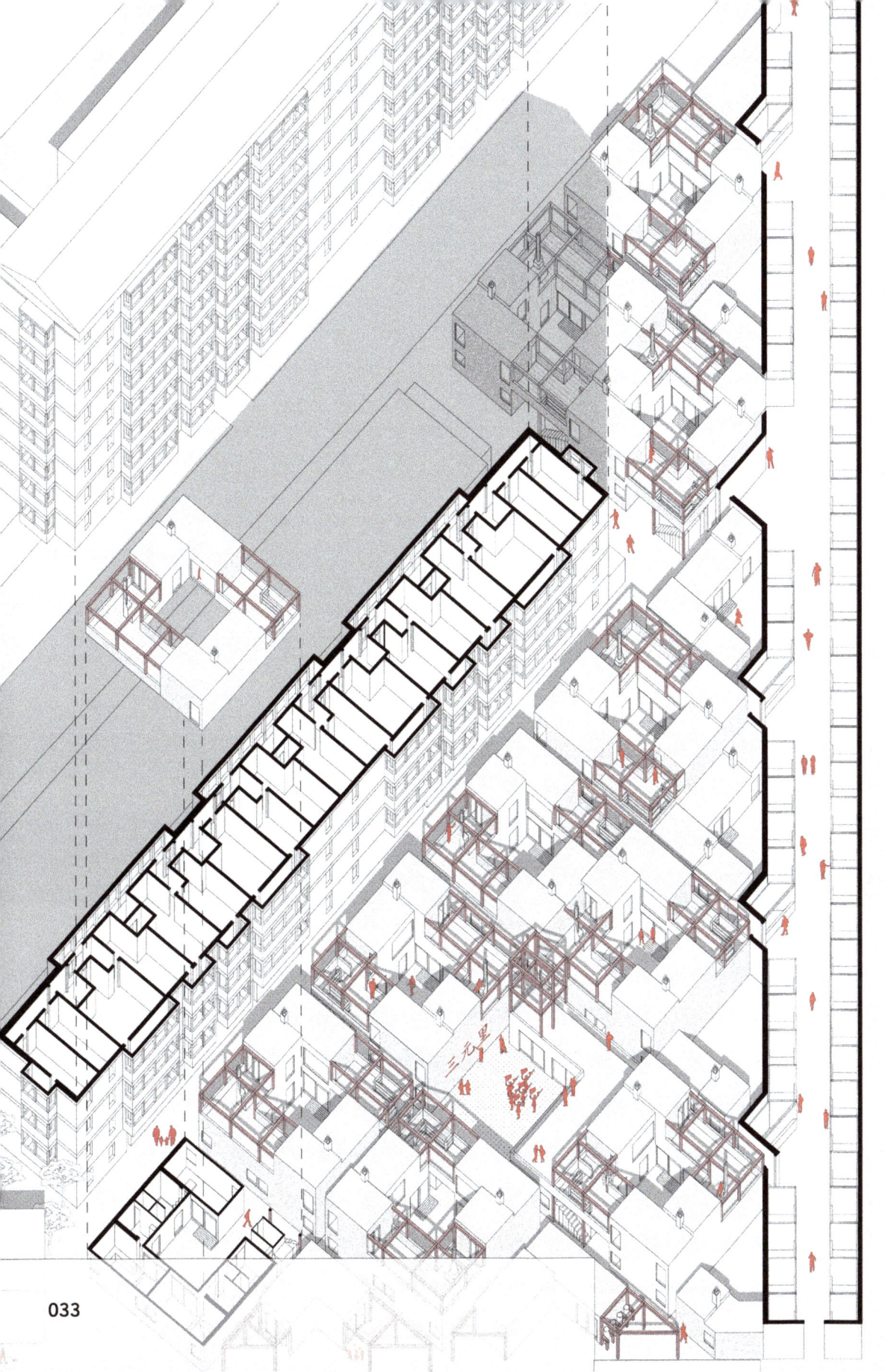

COLLECTIVELY DETACHED

POONAM ALE

LOCATION: SAN YUAN LI, BEIJING, CHINA

In creating a dwelling type of multiple occupancy and shared outdoor spaces for young Beijingers, this project hybridises the courtyard with the detached house.

The primary tectonic approach of this proposal is inspired by Ai Weiwei's artist studio in Caochangdi, which in itself is a re-imagination of the Siheyuan courtyard.

Instead of a four sided enclosure with an open space in the middle, an 'L' shaped spatial configuration moves the open space into the corner of the cubic volume, where it becomes a shared entrance garden. From this arrival space, access is gained to two separate dwellings that are three dimensionally interlocked with each other: a duplex apartment and a maisonette with roof terrace. This volumetric arrangement allows for a even distribution of daylight to each home, and a more dynamic juxtaposition of apartment types, where variation to one does not affect the other. From this one spatial principle, several tectonic iterations can be produced, to create a diverse ensemble of buildings that is read as variations on a theme. As standalone volumes, the proposed buildings can be arranged alongside each other at a variety of spacings to suit different urban contexts, such as those tested here in Sanyuanli, Beijing. The ensemble as a whole creates a rhythmic composition of alleys, streets, boulevards, and squares, offering an urban experience that ranges between intimacy and communal conviviality.

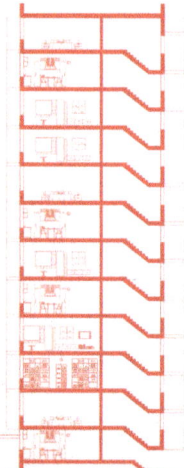

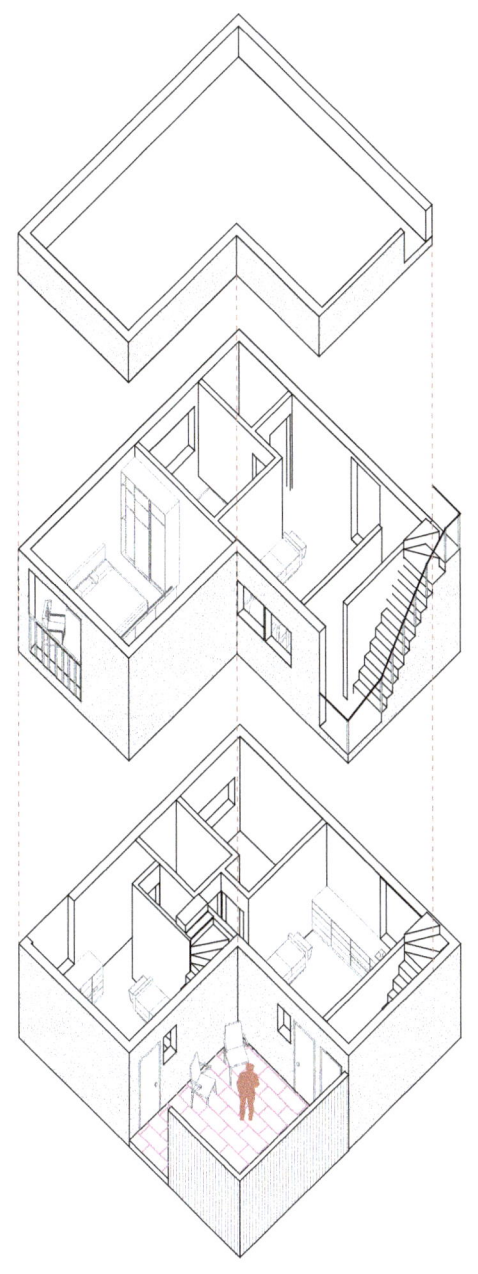

LEARNING LANDSCAPE

MAHEER KHAN

LOCATION: SOMERS TOWN, LONDON, UK

This project inverts the perimeter housing block by pushing the tectonic volumes into the ground and creating a new set of relationships with the street and the public realm.

Developed as a sunken student housing project that would have otherwise occupied a public park, the scheme allows for the roof terraces of the housing in the lowered ground level to become a network of linear public parks at pavement level. This strategy, whose geometry is informed by historic analysis of the site past and pedestrian movement in the present, re-instates the connections and desire lines that the site had previously accommodated, re-providing the wider community with much needed green spaces. From these linear parks one could look down into the sunken gardens, around which the student apartments are arranged. All the apartment are designed as duplexes with tall double height glazed facade that sits behind a high transparency mesh frame acting as a lattice for vegetation to take over. The overall effect is an apartment whose internal atmosphere and environment are modulated throughout the seasons. In the summer the overgrown leaves provides shading, which sheds in the winter to maximise daylight gain into the space. In between the housing are six very different scholars gardens inspired by Baroque sensibilities and use of water, offering the inhabitants a variety of environments, two of which are also accessible by the public.

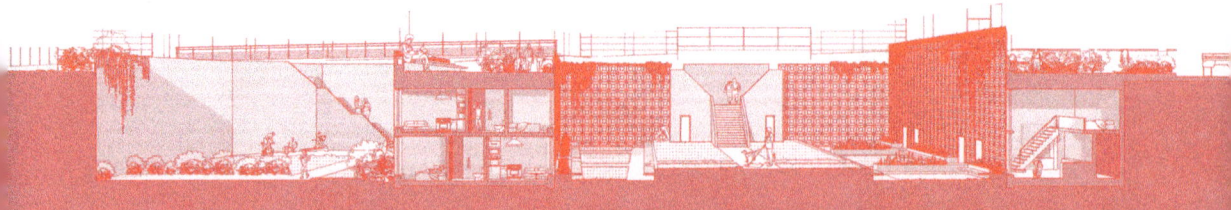

HOMES IN THE LANDSCAPE

YANA STOYANOVA

LOCATION: SOMERS TOWN, LONDON, UK

This project tests the idea that open green spaces and housing are not mutually exclusive, and that the courtyard housing can be integrated into a publicly accessible landscape.

Located within a small under-utilised green space in Somers Town, and heavily influenced by the rammed earth cave dwellings of western China, the proposal introduces housing without compromising on the amount of public green space by pushing the dwellings into the ground, with rooms organised around a sunken courtyard, which provides the residents with daylight and a communal outdoor space. Ponds and rock pools within the courtyard, as well as roof lights bring more light into the rooms, whose walls and roofs become enveloped by earth, providing the building with greater thermal mass, making the dwellings cool in the summer and warm in the winter.

A network of walkways offer access to the sunken apartments from the ground, but also helps to break down the open space into smaller pieces of landscapes with a variety of designations. Some are used as planted borders to provide a sense of privacy to the residential access stair, others become allotments for the residents to tend to, with the rest being freely available to the public as places of rest and play. The gaps between the sunken courtyards are occasionally appropriated to become community libraries and hall for hire.

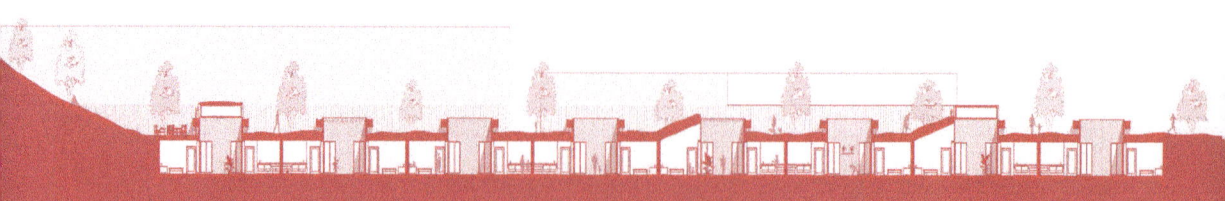

OPEN SIHEYUAN

DREW YATES

LOCATION: FU GUO LI, BEIJING, CHINA

This project reconsiders the relationship between the Siheyuan courtyard and the street, in order to tackle the generous but poorly defined in-between spaces that make up so many of Beijing's slab block housing enclaves.

Whereas the traditional Siheyuan can be said to have its front facing the internal courtyard, and its back facing the Hutong street, and thereby turning its back on the public realm, this project pushes the courtyard onto the street edge and forces the typology to consider the street as a principle facade and frontage.

A pair of multi-generational housing apartments wrap around a shared courtyard entrance facing onto the street. This becomes the arrival space for two households. As the pattern alternate, each household is connect to two neighbours via two courtyards, all facing onto double aspect living rooms. As the spaces becomes more private towards the back, the typology begins to resemble the terrace house arrangement, with bedrooms towards the back and private allotment gardens. A second storey of guest, lodger, or grandparents accommodation gives access to a series of roof terraces.

The urban consequence of this approach is the activation of the street facing facade, into an alternating pattern of opacity and transparency, offering regular glimpses into the heart of this new community from the street.

GARDEN OF MICRO-LIVING

ZIXIAO TONG

LOCATION: SOMERS TOWN, LONDON, UK

This is a radical re-interpretation of the courtyard housing type, in so far that it is an exercise in exploring what the voids between solid built volumes can do.

Intended as an enclave of student housing, the proposal is a seemingly random scattering of minimal cubic housing units across the entirety of the site. Within each cube several students share a set of living room and kitchen. A group of these cubes are then gathered around a shared bath house, also cubic in form. The geometric bringing together of these cubes creates a set of seemingly random voids, which are in fact carefully thought about and calibrated, and act as a re-interpretation of a Chinese scholarly rock garden. Each of these micro-gardens are unique in their sculptural form, becoming framing devices through which the living units are viewed, but also acting as a visual buffers to protect privacy. Connecting these micro gardens into a cohesive route of communal experience is a series of larger indoor/outdoor campus-like programmed spaces, such as amphitheatres, reading pavilions, and sports grounds. This entire ensemble is then surrounded and protected by a perforated garden wall, which modulates the views into and out of the whole community.

From an urban perspective, the site becomes a finely carved out city block that is almost Hutong-like, a labyrinth for chance encounters and communal intimacy.

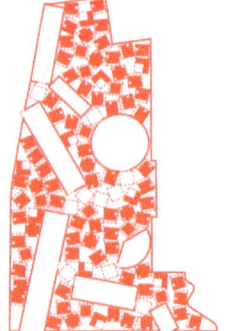 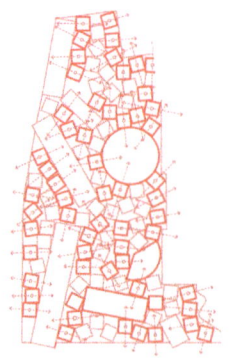 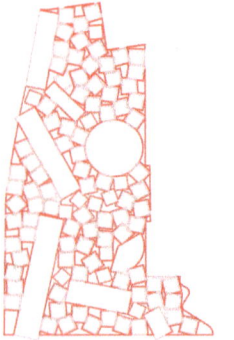 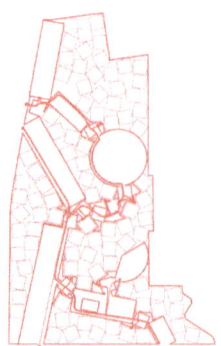

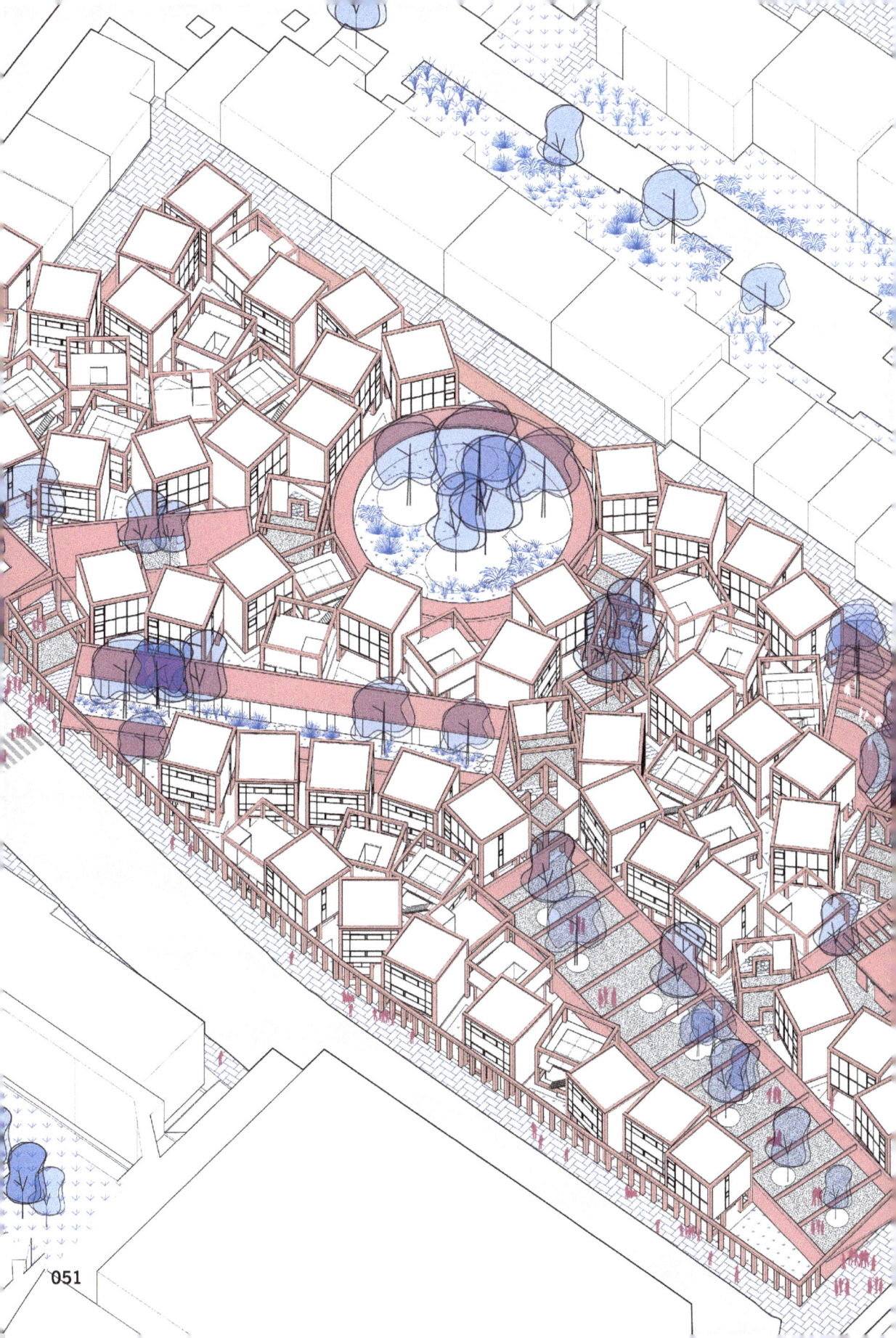

FOLLY FOR A LIVING LANDSCAPE

RYAN MAYERS

LOCATION: SOMERS TOWN, LONDON, UK

This project challenges the conventional co-planar relationship between dwellings and their associated private, communal and public outdoor spaces.

The starting point is once again the Chinese Siheyuan, but instead of discrete households sitting over the ground floor, the proposal imagines a buried typology of 6 private apartments organised around 4 sunken courtyards, accessed via the nexus point where these courtyards meet. This vertical access then grows upwards and becomes a small community pavilion which then serves both the immediate cluster of residents but also a wider neighbourhood of 12 such clusters. Contained within these pavilions on the first floor are tool sheds, visitors apartments, reading rooms, viewing platforms, etc. This three storey structure effectively becomes the heart of each cluster, and a place where residents interact with each other. Taking inspiration from Tschumi's Parc de la Villette, the pavilions are formal variations on a theme which collectively define the formal character of the neighbourhood.

The pavilion at the ground level is buffered by a zone of semi-private/semi-communal landscapes, including allotments, sun-decks, and grey water filtration ponds. The proposals are then intersected by a network of public walkways, pocket green parks, which begin to integrate the proposal with the wider urban context.

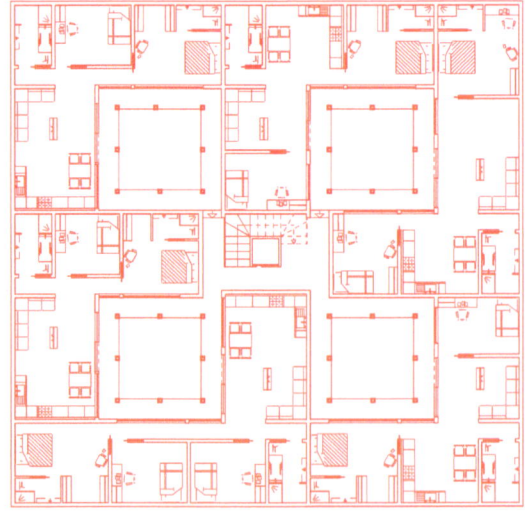

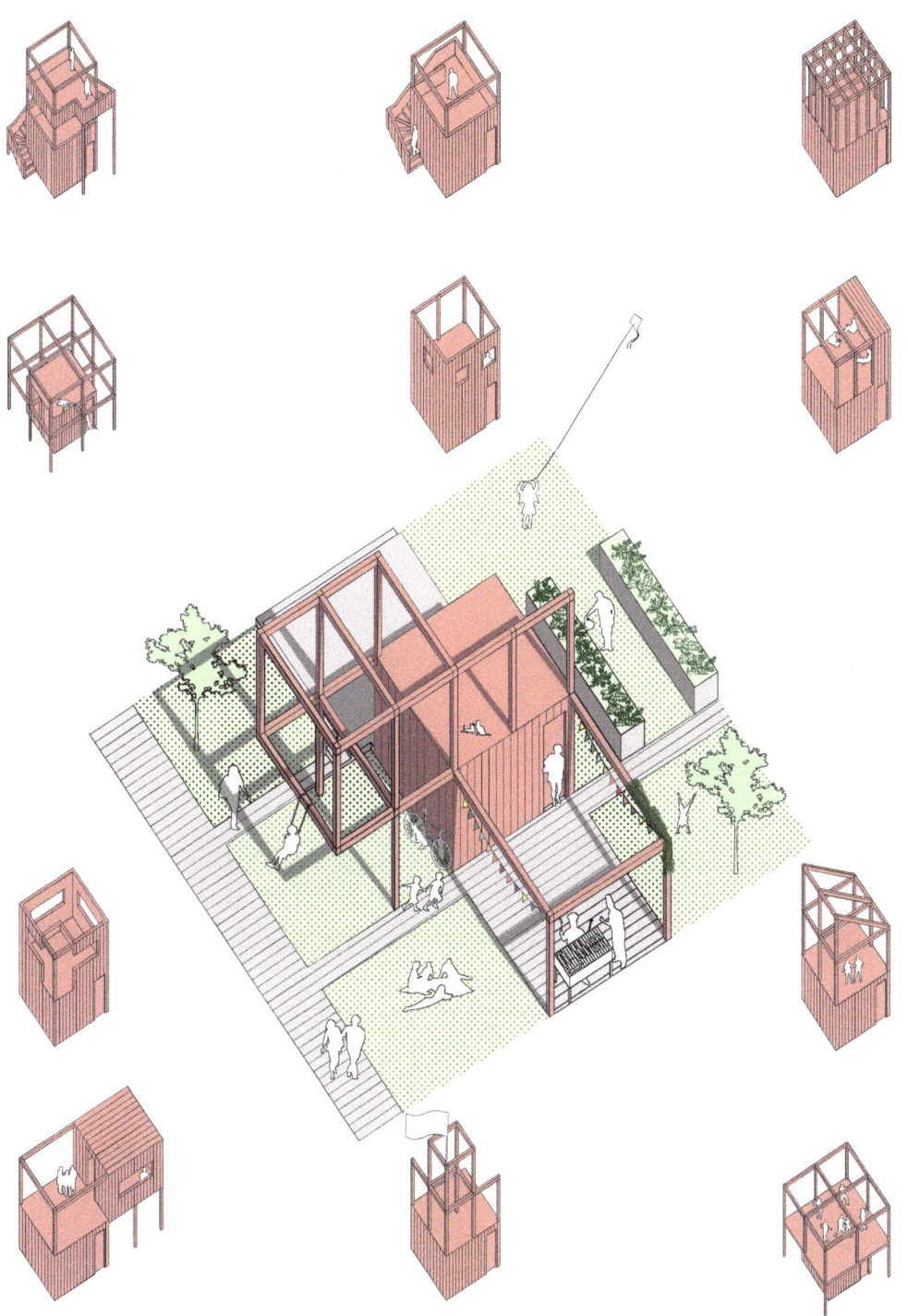

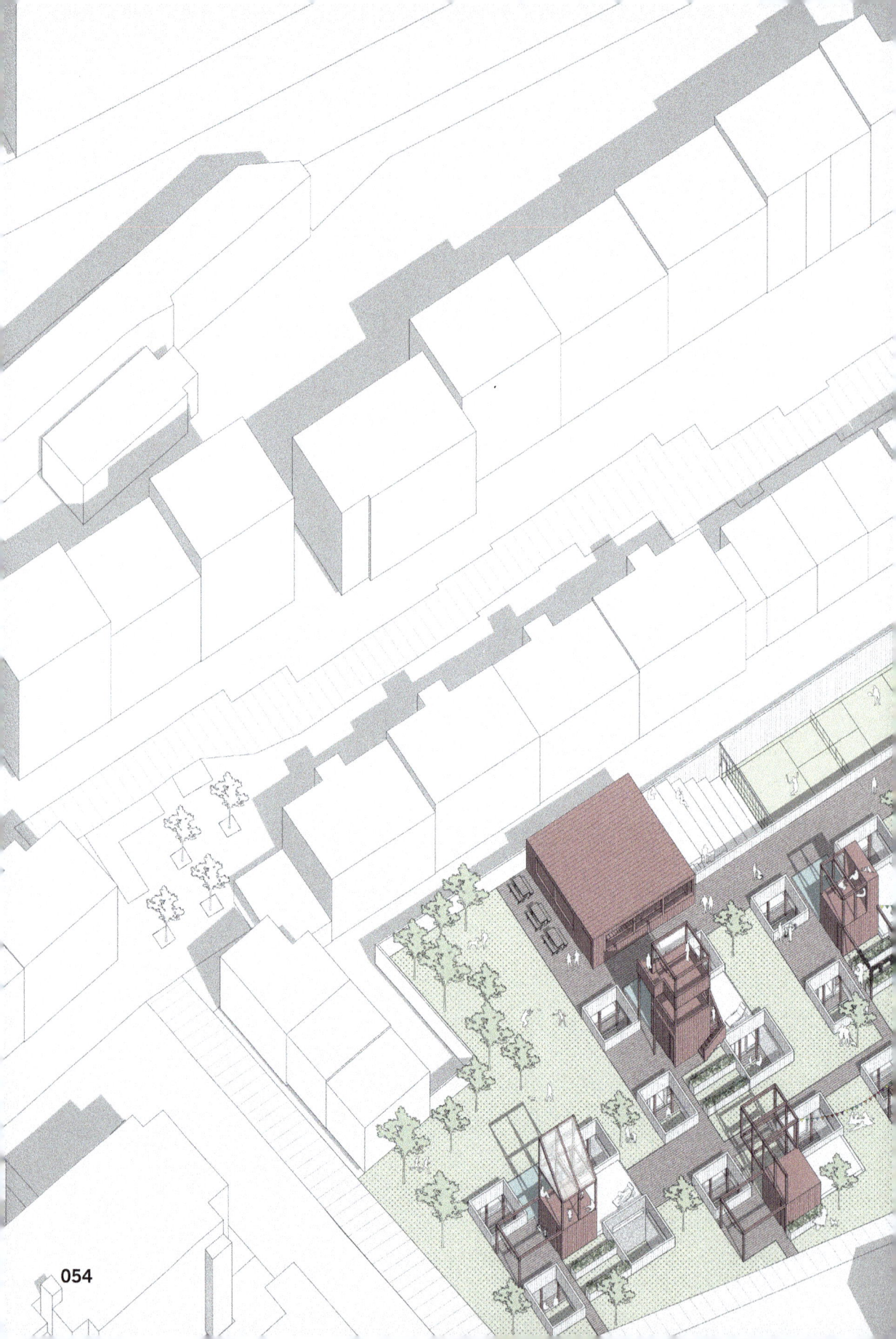

A NEW HUTONG ARCHAEOLOGY

SIGNE PELNE

LOCATION: FU GUO LI, BEIJING, CHINA

This project seeks to revive the spirit of convivial neighbourliness and spatial intimacy which has been lost as the Hutongs and Siheyuans have been replaced with utilitarian slab blocks in Beijing over the past several decades.

Using one such slab block estate in Fu Guo Li as a test bed, the proposal uncovers and re-interprets the historic Hutong and Siheyuan urban pattern that had previously occupied the site, and develops this concept into a sunken infill scheme that address the poorly used and ill defined spaces between the evenly spaced slab housing blocks.

Appearing almost as a piece of archaeology, a series of intersecting alleys are carved into the ground, around which single storey houses for migrants and the elderly are organised. In place of an internally enclosed courtyard, outdoor spaces for these houses take the form of light well gardens, balconies and roof terraces. Bridges linking the roof terraces provides an alternative route for passers by to circumvent this 'archaeological' topography if they so choose. As the alleys rise and fall to traverse these homes, communal spaces, both internal and external are revealed, including a diner, a tea house, and a series of community gardens. The resultant urban experience is one of intensely dynamic and intimate journeys into a closely knit neighbourhood, where there is spatial discovery and delight with every turn of the path.

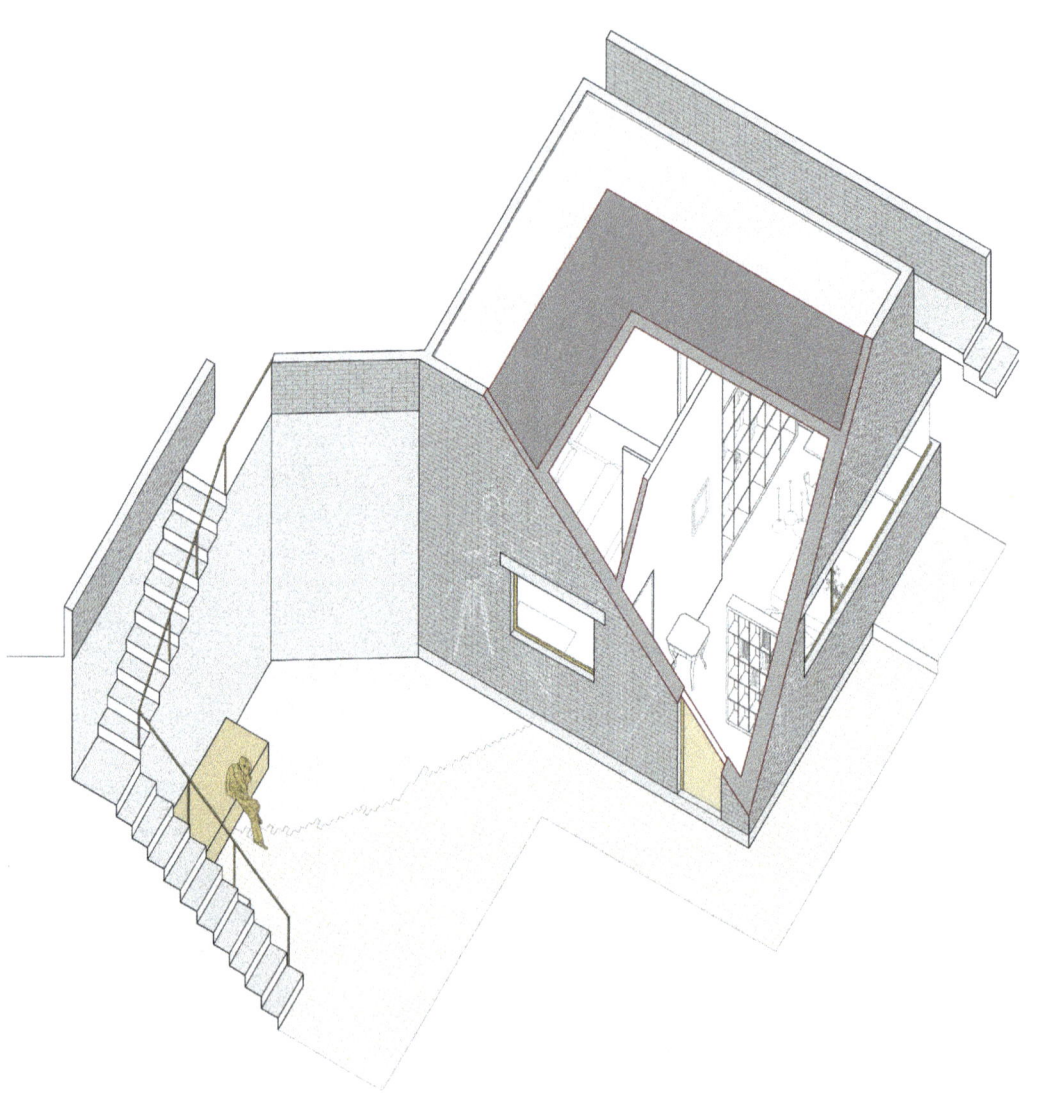

ON HOUSING

KEREN HE, DAVID PORTER, JOHN ZHANG

JZ: The studio in its current form investigates housing design within intensely urban setting in Beijing and London. How was this agenda developed and how has it evolved? Keren, does this have particular relevance and urgency within the context of Chinese urbanity? David, having worked on some of the most important post war housing projects in London, what are your thoughts on the value of investigating housing and neighbourhoods in this comparative manner?

KH: Chinese cities have attracted increasing international attention over the past few decades. People are interested not only in the historical and cultural heritage but also the speed and scale of urbanization and the interaction between traditional and modern lifestyles, which results in unique, complex transformations of urban forms. The impact of communication technology, information exchange, global networks, money flow, and other contemporary phenomenon on how people live in places like Beijing has become a global issue.

To tackle these issues, we at CAFA believe that interdisciplinary and cross-cultural exercises are of vital importance and necessity in design. The experiences of different individuals from our international studio can differ greatly depending on their personal backgrounds. These variables make this international and joint effort in urban programming more interesting and valuable. Additionally, CAFA is a prestigious art academy where architecture students are always exposed to a variety of artistic representations like painting, sculpting, engraving, installation, collages, video, etc. This exposure encourages architecture students to push the boundaries of their work beyond conventional techniques.

DP: We didn't start with the intention of being a housing studio. We were mapping neighbourhoods in areas of change (initially the Ju'er Hutong), trying to understand the overall pattern of habitation and how a new pattern might grow out of the old, seeking what Keren later called the 'poetics of habitation'. We were seeing the city as a place with a living culture rather than a potential building site. And we were working between urban design and architecture but at the domestic scale. At this scale cultural differences between China and Europe are most apparent. So, the design of housing was the outcome of the studio's investigations, rather than its destination.

You mentioned my involvement in housing. As a young

Ju'er Hutong housing by Wu Liangyong, an early experimentation with densifying the Sihueyuan typology

architect in London I had worked for Neave Brown who is now recognised as the most architecturally sophisticated designer of urban housing in the UK. As such, he has become something of a hero to a younger generation of British architects who are starting their careers at a time of 'housing crisis'. I was his 'apprentice' and later his partner – he was a great teacher and I learned much more from him than I did from architecture school. These ideas still influence me.

Neave had been part of a small group of radical architects in the 1960's who were informed by the works of the preceding Team 10 generation. Indeed, Peter Smithson was Neave's final year tutor at the Architectural Association. The architects that followed Team 10 loved the architecture of Le Corbusier, but hated his urbanism – that is to say, they rejected idea that the city and its streets should be demolished in the name of modernism, that modernism should start by wiping the slate clean. Building towers had not been successful in the UK - it became evident very quickly that people found this environment alienating.

So, Neave and his colleagues sought ways of building at high-density but keeping the height low and retaining the pattern of streets, a pattern that people understood. The intention was to build an aesthetically uncompromising modernism that emphasised the organisational and spatial continuity between the new and the old, rather than seeking novel forms that express isolation and separation. I know that you want to ask about 'enclaves' so I'll pick that up later.

JZ: I think on the surface, it may appear at first that the conversation around housing could be quite different between China and the UK, given the differences in geography, climate, construction heritage, material culture, living habits, market forces and social political agencies. However, as human beings, dwelling is a fundamental activity common to us all, despite the differences in how we calibrate the relationship between the inside and the outside, the private and the public, the individual and the communal, etc. Whether in solitude or in the company of others, we all seek shelter from the elements and solace in the idea of the 'home'.

In fact, when one looks really carefully, the very same global forces are asking very similar questions of housing in our cities. Neighbourhoods in Beijing and London are all having to deal with issues of densification, regeneration, and gentrification. As national capitals and global metropolises, London and

A visit with Neave Brown in his Fleet Road flat

Beijing are each having to tackle with the problems of meeting with increasing demand with limited supply of housing. Traditional households based on the family unit are increasingly being replaced with new and more transient forms of co-habitation, enabled by more immaterial technology and networks of social interaction. It's never been more important for architects to be asking questions about housing, particularly when both Beijing and London can each draw on their own rich heritage of post-war social housing programmes.

Despite this urgency, I feel the exploration of housing design at undergraduate level is still surprisingly sparse in the studios of our architecture schools. Rightly or wrongly, our architectural pedagogy has come to fetishize the 'brief'. Students are attracted by the glamour of some hitherto unimagined combination of 'programmes' which demand some novel tectonic. Housing design, on the other hand demands technical rigour and poetic imagination at the same time, a much more challenging undertaking for students. This makes our collective pursuit in the studio all the more prescient.

JZ: Another particular focus of the studio within the realm of housing design, has been the interrogation of how different groups of people might come to share their lives together, in some cases this has been referred to as 'collective housing'. What are your thoughts on the relevance of this theme in context of the shifting patterns of urban living in places like Beijing and London? Keren, what has been the history of collective housing in China, and what of the recent emergence of 'knowledge workers' in places like Beijing? David, can one bring post war social housing in the UK into this contemporary conversation on collective living, and what are we to make of the resurgent interest in the work and idealism of that era?

KH: Mass housing or social housing in Mainland China started in the early 20th century but was not fully developed until after the new era of the People's Republic of China in the late 1940s and early 1950s. In a way comparable to the West after the world wars, the development of mass housing in China was spurred by a growing population and social change. In Mainland China from the 1950s until the 1980s, the socialist government that controlled the land began to build mass housing to provide for the growing population. There were the so-called "Workers' Village" (gongren xincun) which were first built nationwide in 1950s. The average area for such a "village" is approximately 30-60 hectares, and the layout of the houses was greatly influenced by Soviet-style housing planning. From the '50s until the '80s a lot of effort was devoted to designing and mass producing low-budget prototype housing. In Beijing, the state-owned BIAD (Beijing Institute of Architectural Design) established a special department that has been designing prototype housing since the 1950s. For instance, in 1955 a series of houses were designed on an extremely low budget for co-living families, with shared kitchens and toilets. In the early '80s, the department developed prototypes such as the typical slab plan and tower plan, which were dominant in Mainland China for decades. After the 1980s, these housing prototypes became the first experiments for the open housing market. Residents who lived in these houses could pay an affordable price to transfer housing ownership. But after the market opened fully in the 1990s, privately owned real estate gradually rose to become the major force it continues to be today. In today's overwhelming real estate housing market, planning for affordable housing in terms of policy, design, and distribution is still quite premature. As part of our studio's study, we are focusing on the renewal of the prototype housing community that developed in the 80s and 90s. These communities have experienced a decline in building quality and neighbourhood environment with unprecedented high housing prices, complicated demographics and social structures, and tumultuous transformations.

In the studio program the students normally work on designing collective housing for a chosen site. In this case, it is vitally important to address who the residents will be. The new urban program strategy can be aimed at different resident groups, such as migrate workers, senior citizens, or the young people who we dubbed "knowledge workers". Through their design practice, the students need to investigate and think in-depth about historical, social, and economic contexts to create responsible solutions for a sustainable environment, build a healthy and dynamic community, explore urban lifestyles and housing typology, consider flexibility and future changes, arrange necessary public uses and spaces into the new development, pay attention to the relationship between the public and private, and address building technology with a consideration of sustainable modern technology and regional tradition.

DP: This is a difficult and very political question. After the second World War the UK established a 'welfare state' to provide health services, pensions and social security for all. Housing was built by local authorities, subsidised by the government. Originally this 'council

A typical Beijing residential enclave built in the early 1990s in Fu Guo Li

housing' was provided for a wide range of the population, and not just the poor, but key workers that each city needed to function such as schoolteachers, policemen, bus drivers etc. In this period in the United Kingdom, as in China, architects were anonymous, working for local or regional government: they were not star-architects. This was the period when Neave Brown was most active – he was not running his own practice but was a local government official (not very glamorous!). In this period most graduating architects in the UK found work in this way, building council housing, new schools, new universities and new towns, often working directly for the government.

The first big change was the invention of what we now call 'social housing' when councils were stopped from building for a wide population to concentrate on providing for the neediest in society. Although this seemed logical it meant that those people with the most problems were concentrated together. Council housing projects became what Keren calls 'enclaves' – clearly defined districts with concentrations of people who were poor, often unemployed, suffering from family breakdown, and mental health problems, housed together in noticeably modern architecture! In the public mind modern architecture became associated with social breakdown.

The government then stopped Council housing altogether to encourage everyone to own their own home. Councils were forced to sell the properties they had built but could not reinvest the profits to build more. Things got worse as the government shifted resources into homes built by private developers who had no experience of city-building but made their money building large estates of small suburban houses outside the core of the city. Densities were dropped and car dependency increased.

The population of London had decreased steadily after the war, but in the 1980's, just when densities were dropping, the population began to steadily rise again as London began to attract workers from Europe and beyond. This unplanned growth created a housing crisis. It was made worse because the homes sold, so that people could become property owners, were often quickly resold at a profit, where people increasing saw a home as an investment. And so, capital started to flow into London to fuel a rising property market, making new homes progressively unaffordable, particularly for the young.

This is the problem we now face. The good news is a revived interest in how we might live an urban life at reasonable density, where people feel that they are members of society not just individuals. Facing this challenge has led the new generation to look back to the pioneering housing projects of the 1960's such as those by Neave Brown and Local Councils have again become active in building housing.

JZ: Indeed, the works of Neave's generation is enjoying somewhat of a renaissance at the moment. We are seeing a resurgence of councils in London more willing to undertake the design and delivery of social housing again, and more willing to retain in-house architects again. The Stirling Prize, the highest honour for a building in the UK was won by a social housing project in Norwich in 2019. There is a real wind change.

On the other hand, collective housing in China draws on a slightly different utopian heritage. As Keren mentioned, the collectivisation movement in its heydays in the 1950s created a lot of interesting prototypes of co-living. For example, the large Fusuijing Building near Baitasi in Beijing was a fascinating experiment in collectivised living, where the apartments had no kitchens and all 358 households ate together in a shared canteen. Projects such as these were very much a product of their time. However, critical re-examination of collective living in academia and practice are never too far from us, the research work of P.V. Aureli and Liu Jiankun's recent West Village in Chengdu are interesting sources of re-imaginations of collective life.

Additionally, I think there is now a convergence of renewed interest in 'collective living', in both China and the West, which sits outside of the 'social housing' framework. This time, the communist ideals of a communal living have been appropriated by capitalism. Using the same lexicon that evokes a romantic sense of collective identity and togetherness, real estate developers have created housing developments of minimal private spaces with supposed 'shared facilities', to cater for a generation of mobile and transient young people living, working and studying in our cities, who already live in non-familial based arrangements. The YOU+ 'communities' in Beijing and 'The Collective Old Oak' in London are just two such examples. The global resonance of these tendencies is a vindication of the studio's pursuit of collective housing as an endeavour.

HOUSING IN SECTION

DOUGLAS MURPHY

EVANS & SHALEV AND NETWORKS OF EXPERIMENTATION IN POST-WAR LONDON HOUSING DESIGN

The production of housing architecture in the UK is in a contradictory situation. Contemporary design is highly constrained by market forces, from apartment layouts to densities and specifications. But there is simultaneously a sustained interest within the profession for a period of production after the Second World War where architects had more capacity to experiment with the design of dwellings, with the result being some highly celebrated landmarks in the history of public housing.

This essay will examine flows of information that helped to produce new housing design in that era, asking how networks of teaching, publication and collaboration came together to bring innovative ideas into the field. By focusing attention on a particular unbuilt housing project from the mid-1960s, some of these issues can be examined. What were the preoccupations of the architects of the period? How did they learn their technique, and how was this refined? How did they develop ideas outside of practice, and how were these concepts brought to fruition? And are there meaningful comparisons to be made with the situation in the present day?

One of the defining issues in the UK built environment is a severe and persistent housing crisis. In recent decades the monetary value of houses, especially in the economically prominent southeast of England, has risen far more quickly than wages have grown, a consequence of an intense demand that is being largely unmet by current supply rates. Houses are increasingly commodified on a growing international market, and have been transformed into financial assets in a way not seen in previous generations.

The design and construction of new housing is largely controlled by a small number of large builders, and a substantial proportion of this production is of a highly generic product designed for suburban areas, with a small selection of easily built house types lightly customized, and thought to be tailored to the needs and desires of buyers' lifestyles. In more central locations the output is by necessity more architecturally complicated, but the guiding principles of residential development are still highly constrained.

New urban residential design is similarly restricted. Density is increased to the highest possible intensity that will receive statutory approval. Apartment layouts and types are generic and rarely subject to innovation, specifications are rigorously controlled. In order to reduce financial risk, sites are divided by developers into separate plots the size of the largest practical single building, each of which can be developed distinctly and by a separate design and construction team.

As a result, housing makes up a large part of the output of the contemporary architectural profession, but the scope for action is limited. Architects have responsibilities for urban qualities – massing, facades, planning in general – but historically speaking the parameters of the housing product are mostly fixed.

At the same time, a concurrent development has been a lack of focus on housing in the pedagogical context. Over the last few decades architectural education has by and large become much more experimental, with a now long-established tradition of 'paper architecture' existing with its own set of concerns and norms outside of the professional milieu. In this context studying housing design becomes seen as technical, difficult, and perhaps even boring, and it makes up a small part of current student output.

One result of the current crisis is a widespread nostalgia for the housing of the post-WWII period, a generation when there was a far higher level of production, roughly equally split between the private and the public sector. The significant presence of the social democratic state in the sector at the time allowed for a greater level of innovation and experimentation, with the profit motive a less significant factor in the creation of new housing architecture.

In the context of today's strangled housing market, and a variety of expulsion and dispersal stories related to redevelopment, there is an increasingly widespread nostalgia for a time when housing was produced in a more benevolent fashion. Where recent decades have seen major controversies on formal, aesthetic, political or economic grounds, and while huge numbers of houses have been demolished long before their originally expected obsolescence, recent years have seen a noticeable swing in British public consciousness towards an appreciation of modernist housing, which is at least in part because of its social intentions as well as its spatial qualities.

In the UK, the most significant and increasingly celebrated product of the post-war housing industry is the work of what is known as "Cook's Camden", a series of public housing estates created by the London Borough of Camden's Architect's Department from the mid-1960s until the end of the 1970s. The most emphatically modernist public housing built in the UK, they are increasingly celebrated for their architectural ambitions and public spirit:

for example, Neave Brown (1929-2018), one of Camden's principle architects, was awarded the 2018 RIBA Royal Gold Medal in recognition of this work.

The work of Cook's Camden is significant for being based upon the concept of "low-rise, high density", which was a rejection of the standard practice of building high-rise residential blocks. Instead, Cook's Camden drew inspiration equally from worldwide avant-garde practice and from London's traditional terraced housing models, in the process creating a synthesis of modernist environments which were still recognisably street-based urbanism.

The network which produced the Camden School of architecture, among other projects of the time, is equally significant. The architects involved were often young, having only recently graduated from their studies, and they were entrusted to lead projects of complexity and scale that very rarely happens today. The work itself was experimental, featuring innovations that in many cases meant that the projects were prototypes, without previously built precedent. Thus the ways in which information was passed on and ideas were developed is of substantial interest.

The Camden School itself has received much attention in recent years, with the primary estates of Alexandra Road, Fleet Road, Branch Hill, Highgate New Town, Mansfield Road and Maiden Lane all receiving attention. Each of these estates can be understood as something of a variation on a set of themes, including stepped sections, free plans with moving partitions, outdoor rooms, pedestrian and vehicle segregation, within the broader "low-rise high-density" concept. Aesthetically the estates all experimented with a repertoire of triangular shapes, concrete and white render, with ply- and softwood joinery inside.

This consistency is both historically and aesthetically satisfying, but it makes understanding the work in its context more difficult. Camden Council were blessed with high tax revenues and political ambitious politicians, which partly explains the high quality of the delivered projects but also explains the apparent isolation of the work compared to other local authorities and developers of the time. However the projects of the Camden School are only a small amount of the experimental housing architecture being designed in the UK (and beyond) at that point, which remained unbuilt by the time the political mood changed in the late 1970s.

One example of a project whose construction would have been an important contribution to the housing architecture of the period was the project for Broadclyst Village, designed by Eldred Evans & David Shalev. On the one hand it is an inconsequential footnote, but at the same time under examination its significance as architecture in terms of its influence as a work of research and development becomes clear, shedding light on the intersections of practice, pedagogy and research.

In 1965, a competition was held to develop housing on land in the village of Broadclyst in the southwest of England. The land had been in the ownership of the Acland family, attached to their country house Killerton, which had been given to the National Trust in the general wave of donations around the end of WWII. The competition envisaged an extension of the existing village through the construction of 280 homes, and invited entries from teams led by contractors.

There were sixteen entries to the competition, which was won by the team led by Richard Barry, First Avenue Construction Company, who were employing the architects H. Werner Rosenthal with Denis Gailey, Eldred Evans and David Shalev. Evans and Shalev were professional and domestic partners, and the design was later attributed to them together.

The site was an undulating patch of open ground surrounded by a loose collection of traditional houses, and the architects proposed, counter to a low-density suburban or rural collection of detached dwellings, to run the accommodation across the site in a series of repeated high-density 'clusters'. Three of these were effectively identical, with those at either end adjusted slightly to end conditions.

The development was to be largely three storeys high: a lower level which was accessible to vehicles, a segregated pedestrian level with its own access to the dwellings, and an upper level purely of accommodation. The construction was concrete cross wall construction, a common choice for low-rise high-density designs, and the typical dwelling featured kitchen spaces opening up to the gardens on the lowest floor, bedrooms at the top of the dwelling, and living spaces in between.

What was innovative about the competition winning design was the complexity of the dwelling in section. Behind the facade facing the exterior, the living space was pulled back to create a double height space above the front of the kitchen, while at the rear of the living space a void above created another double height volume, which was to be located underneath a large roof light. This would not only bring light deep into the dwelling, allowing for a room to focus towards or away from the depths, but it also created

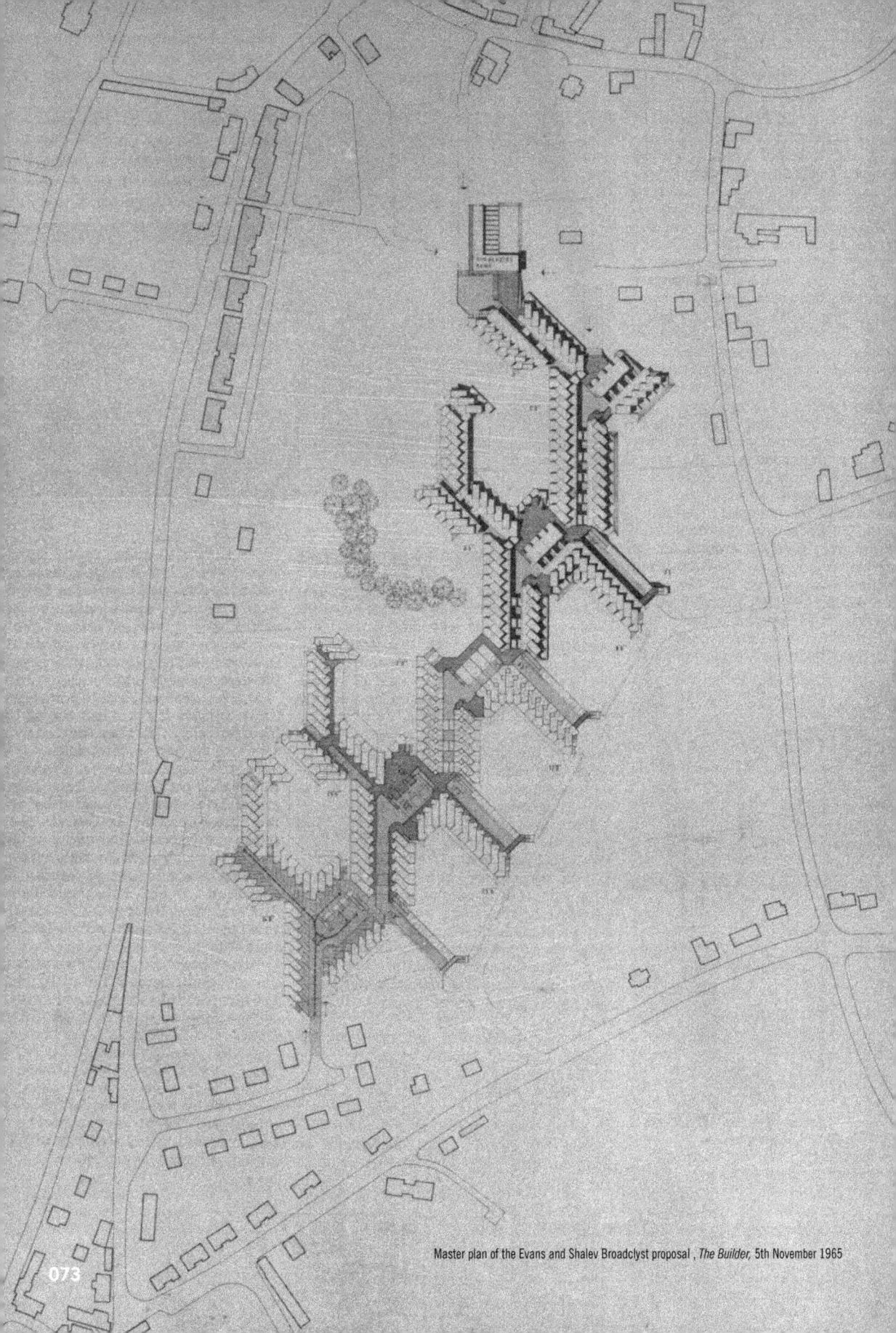

Master plan of the Evans and Shalev Broadclyst proposal, *The Builder,* 5th November 1965

Physical model of proposed housing type, *Architectural Review,* January 1966

a free flowing sense of space throughout the volume as a whole.

Sources for the scheme could be found in Siedlung Halen by Atelier 5, a highly celebrated project which deeply influenced radical British housing design, while the details shown in drawings seem to derive from the English industrial aesthetic of early works by James Stirling. The clustering of the houses, whereby certain forms repeated at different scales, shows the influence of Aldo van Eyck and Herman Hertzberger and other Team 10 architects.

The houses designed by Evans and Shalev were innovative, but were somewhat inefficient, with large amounts of space lost to voids and loosely defined space, and the competition assessors made recommendations for improvement. A new, amended scheme was published in November of 1965, by which point the project had changed significantly.

The most obvious difference between the two schemes was in orientation. The first scheme was staggered across the site but was thoroughly orthogonal, but the new scheme now ran across a set of 45° changes in angle. This was ostensibly to improve access for vehicles and parking, but it allowed for a significant experiment in the plan of the houses, which now ran between cross walls which turned diagonally one way and then back through the depth of the house.

Scheme two increased the spatial efficiency of the dwellings through an even more complex sectional arrangement. The lowest floor, at road level, had storage and a staircase running up into the house. The half-level above had the living room opening out to the garden, and another half staircase connected to a bathroom and kitchen looking out over the pedestrian street. A dining space looked down into the living room, but was situated under a void, again lit by a roof light. A half-level rise gave access to a master bedroom, and a further half-level rise led to a bathroom and two more bedrooms, oriented 45° from the rest of the house.

This increased complexity enabled the house to achieve an even more sophisticated level of volumetric richness, with most rooms spatially connected to the central void throughout. The top light made a deeper plan possible, while also meaning that the house could be oriented in a number of directions without it losing clarity as a form, a very different approach to orientation from much contemporary practice which tended to orientate buildings directly to south light or as east-west facing depending on function.

The spatial fluidity implied by these half-levels and variety of light sources should be understood as being in step with changing attitudes to domesticity. Experiments in the counter-culture notwithstanding, modernist housing design was at this point altering relationships between spaces in the home, moving children's bedrooms away from parents, blurring the boundaries between kitchen spaces and living areas and loosening the specificity of leisure spaces within the home. The scheme for Broadclyst shows an example of this kind of design thinking, where notions of free-plan developed in a previous generation began to intersect with domestic emancipation and increased leisure.

After scheme two was published, the Broadclyst housing scheme was not developed further. The site was eventually built upon in the early 1980s, with architecturally unremarkable semi-vernacular housing that nevertheless in places appears to mimic the angled planning of the original Evans Shalev scheme.

The ideas developed in the Broadclyst housing proposal would be developed further by the architects. Their proposal (also unbuilt) for a block of housing association apartments in Camden Square (1968) continued to develop the top-lit terrace concept, and managed to stack split-section apartments above each other in a surprisingly convincing way, with a variety of unique plan types. This scheme abandoned the 45 degree planning of Broadclyst scheme two but included ideas drawn from the rectilinear cluster blocks of scheme one.

Evans & Shalev would eventually get an opportunity to test some of their ideas about clustering and complex sectional development in two projects that they built as part of the Alexandra Road Estate, whose main housing, designed by Neave Brown, is the most famous work of Cooks Camden. Evans & Shalev's home for severely disabled people, opening in 1979, had a plan thoroughly broken up into object clusters repeating at different rhythms across the site, while their home for disabled children elsewhere on the estate featured a bedroom block with clear similarities to the Broadclyst split-section. Both of these projects still exist but have both been altered greatly, and are both in different use to what they were originally built for.

That Evans & Shalev would build two of their very rare early works for Camden Council demonstrates the interrelated professional and educational networks of the time. One particularly significant network was the firm of Lyons Israel Ellis, founded in the early 1930s. This practice, who built many housing and educational buildings after WWII, were incubators of a number of talented British architects in the late 1950s and early 1960s, including James Stirling and James Gowan, Alan Colquhoun and John Miller, or Richard MacCormac. Neave Brown and Eldred Evans worked there at the same time, during which time they would have learned how to use concrete as a sculptural material, for which Lyons Israel Ellis were renowned, and which would be an important part of both architects early work. This connection with Neave Brown was important in bringing Evans & Shalev to Camden Council's attention.

Educational connections were vital as well. Evans taught architecture at the Regent Street Polytechnic (now the University of Westminster), while Shalev taught at the Architectural Association, as did Neave Brown. The AA was a significant source of recruits to Camden Council, not least because the office and school were around the corner from each other. During the mid 1960s Shalev taught the architects Gordon Benson and Alan Forsyth, who were hired by Camden Council after graduating, and worked directly for Neave Brown on Alexandra Road. Benson & Forsyth were responsible for three of the 'great' Camden Council estates, Branch Hill, Gospel Oak and Maiden Lane, and in each of these projects the influence of Evans & Shalev's work at Broadclyst can be discerned.

The split-section experiments of Broadclyst were not entirely unique to Evans & Shalev. Apartments known as 'scissor-section', which ascended by half-level and could eliminate a corridor on every other floor of a tower block

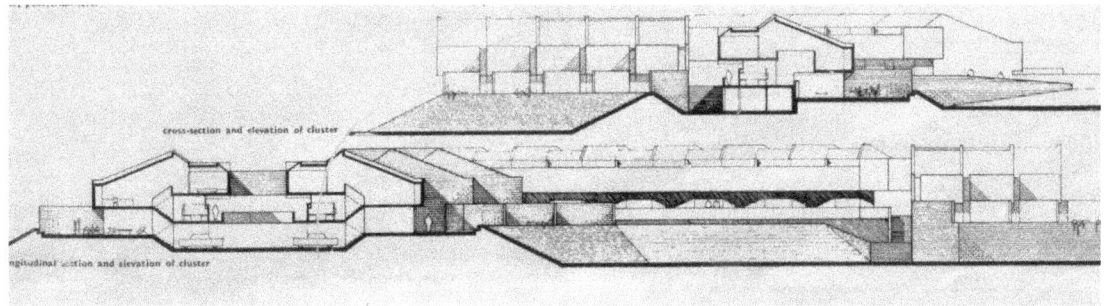

Section through Evan and Shalev's Broadclyst proposal, *Architectural Review*, January 1966

Computer rendering of the view from master bedroom of a typical flat, image by the author

were experimented with by Kenneth Frampton working for Douglas Stephen & Partners in an apartment block in London completed in 1964. Neave Brown later included apartments with a split level in Fleet Road and Alexandra Road, where a half-level change allowed for a 1.5 height living room, a generosity of volume largely absent from mass-housing of the period.

But at Branch Hill, designed in 1968, Benson & Forsyth created apartments spread across half levels, the uppermost of which had roof lights and a void above the dining spaces below. Branch Hill's domestic plans were clearly derived from Broadclyst, in particular having dining spaces connected to the kitchen but situated directly under a central void, and borrowing the strict half-level arrangement intensified Neave Brown's previous experiments in split-level apartments.

Furthermore, Branch Hill's formal arrangement was heavily influenced by Evans & Shalev's Newport High School, their only significant early work, where within an immediately non-urban environment a natural slope was utilised to 'step' the building down the landscape, with sub-buildings laid out on strictly clustered grids. Later projects, in particular Benson & Forsyth's schemes in Gospel Oak, saw central roof lights as the spatial focus of narrow, deep cross wall plans laid out over multiple and stacked half-levels, and were essentially constructed examples of types that had originated but remained on Evans & Shalev's drawing boards.

This experimentalism was relatively short-lived, as the favourable financial and political conditions did not last long. A later derivation of the Broadclyst-Branch Hill terrace type Benson & Forsyth designed for the Gospel Oak estate, built to a more restricted budget, retained its roof light but lost its split levels, in the process becoming a far more conventional apartment type, which nevertheless was heavily criticised when the estate suffered severe decline in the 1980s.

Architects were forced to adapt to changing circumstances – local authorities were effectively prevented from housing development by the mid 1980s, so architects had to move into alternative fields. Evans and Shalev developed an idiom with greater reference to historic form, and their later buildings were civic in stature and widely understood to be postmodern in intellectual approach, although spatial complexity remained a hallmark of projects such as Tate St Ives, completed in 1991.

Housing designed largely in section became harder to achieve. For reasons partly described above, new urban housing tended towards 'block' types, forms which permit very little complexity in section, partly due to the impossibility of drawing light into deep buildings, but also due to the increased costs of complicated structures. Higher overall housing densities also mean that area lost to spatial complexity represents a significant loss to the overall return value of the developments. Furthermore, the relative lack of innovation in terrace-type development also mitigates against developments based on unchanging sections 'extruded' across plans.

However, there are signs that within the UK market it is still possible for sectional design to be part of the production of housing. Sectional design is valuable in low-energy housing design, with orientation to and away from certain directions of sunlight providing heat regulation effects, and this may become a greater part of housing design depending upon how energy related issues develop. Sectional design also plays an important role in the output of boutique developer Solidspace, whose upmarket apartments take advantage of the complexities of split sections to improve the perceived volume and luxuriousness of their product. Furthermore, the split section is becoming part of the educational landscape again, in large part due to the gradual reappearance of housing as a research project within architectural education. Student groups study and visit the more advanced post-war housing estates in increasing numbers, and this research is beginning to appear in the work of practitioner/academics such as MAE, albeit in small cases and at the more 'boutique' end of the market.

Douglas Murphy *is an architect, writer and educator. He is the author of the books 'Last Futures' and 'The Architecture of Failure'. He studied at the Glasgow School of Art and the Royal College of Art. Having previously worked for Lynch Architects, he is now the MA Architecture ADS1 Studio Master at the Royal College of Art. He is the 'architecture correspondent' at Icon magazine, as well as writing for a wide range of publications on architecture, fine art and photography. He has taught and lectured at Oxford University, UCL, The Royal College of Art, The Architectural Association, ETH Zurich, Historical Materialism Conference, The London Art Fair and London Design Festival among others, and has appeared on BBC Radio and Frieze TV.*

Computer rendering of the view from the external yard, image by the author

TERRACES

JOHN ZHANG

Typically understood as dwellings attached to each other and arranged in a row, terraces can be found across the world, but is particularly prominent in the UK. If Beijing's traditional urban form is defined by the Siheyuan courtyard dwellings and the mat urban pattern, then London is shaped by its rows of terraces.

Through the simplicity of its spatial order and the intrinsic qualities of its tectonics, the terrace house is incredibly robust and adaptable to changing patterns of living: from housing the nobility with lived in servants in the 19th Century to co-habiting individuals in the 21st Century. As it turns out, when rooms are generously proportioned and well lit, there are very few functions it cannot successfully accommodate. The terrace typology is also deceptively low rise and high density. The Georgian terraces present a three storey principal street facade, but a raised ground floor allows for an additional lower ground basement to be created, and the roof attic often contains a dormer or mansard floor. The humble Victorian terrace has the same density as many of the high rise tower blocks of 1950s and 60s in the UK, which were built to replace terrace housing.

Perhaps most importantly, the terraced house has the ability to create a street based urbanism. With a strong sense of front and back, its principal facade faces the street, and the street is both activated and overlooked by the rhythmic repetition of entrances and living rooms. Thus the relationship between house and street is much more interactive, to see and be seen. The uniformity of a rhythmically repetitive facade also means that an entire row of terrace houses can be compositionally considered as a coherent and continuous street experience. This is evident in the compositions of Carlton House Terrace and York Terrace, both by Nash, where the totality of the entire terrace is considered as an ensemble and composed as such. It is precisely these qualities of the terrace house typology that led Neave Brown's generation to rethink the high rise tower block approach to housing in the 1950s.

Projects such as Alexandra Road Estate by Neave Brown, Branch Hill by Benson and Forsyth, and Polygon Estate by Peter Tabori were all results of this rapprochement with the terrace house, in creating a modernist low rise high density street based urbanism.

Whilst the terraced house is not native to China, a significant British colonial legacy has influenced Chinese variations and hybrids of the terrace housing type, the most recognised of which is the Shanghai Shikumen terraces, which are narrow two storey houses attached and arranged in a row. Whereas the London terrace is accessed off the street, each Shikumen house fronts onto and is accessed via a narrow alley known as a Longtang, whose intimate scale and somewhat communal atmosphere is at once reminiscent of both the Beijing Hutongs and the London Mews, but is nevertheless public. Shikumen house has a hard paved and high walled front yard, a hybrid of the London terrace front garden and the Siheyuan courtyard. Where the English terrace backs onto private gardens, the Shikumen houses exit onto a rear alley, but have a first floor roof terrace instead. The Shikumen is a demonstration of how the street based urbanism of the terrace typology evolved and adapted meaningfully to different climatic, geographical, social and cultural contexts.

The work shown in this section from the students very much continues this line of enquiry, with various re-imaginings of the terrace or row typology. Of particular note is Ryan Speer's uncovering of a unique Georgian terrace type with shared entrances, which was used as a point of departure to create a programmatically complex and tectonically sophisticated collections of homes within the traditional envelopes of terrace houses. For the others, the terrace typology was augmented to accommodate multi-generational and shared living, added to existing buildings to create live work homes, or hybridised with gardens and courtyards.

TERRACE RE-IMAGINED

RYAN SPEER

LOCATION: SOMERS TOWN, LONDON, UK

This is a daring re-imagination of the terrace house that unleashed the typology's potential to accommodate the increasingly complex arrangements of contemporary co-habitation.

The project is informed by a rich set of historic research into the polygon estate in Somers Town, which at one point was the site for a rare circular shaped Georgian terrace with shared porches between two households and a communal garden in the centre of the circle. This idea of shared spaces led to the development of a novel terrace typology in which five different apartment types are brought together: family homes, student dorms, young couple's duplexes, key worker housing, and bachelor lofts. The lives of this diverse group of inhabitants are enhanced through a series of shared spaces: from basement leisure suites, to the large entrance lobby; from triple height winter-gardens, to mid-level reading spaces; from shared roof terrace to the large rear communal garden. Sectionally, the alternating apartments and shared spaces create a complex and rich interior experience, whilst navigating level changes against the street and the rear garden to preserve privacy, maximise daylight and maintain visual and physical access. From an urban perspective, the rhythmic repetition of the carefully composed brick facade offer glimpses of the shared interior space and rear garden and creates a dynamic street experience for the public.

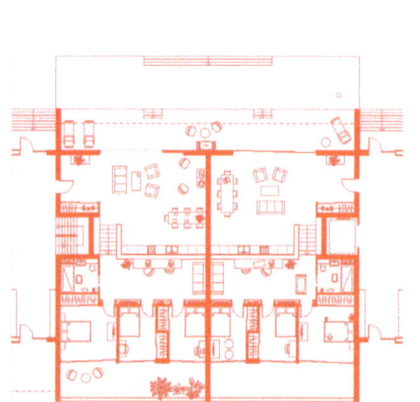
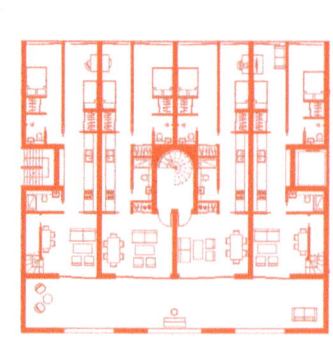
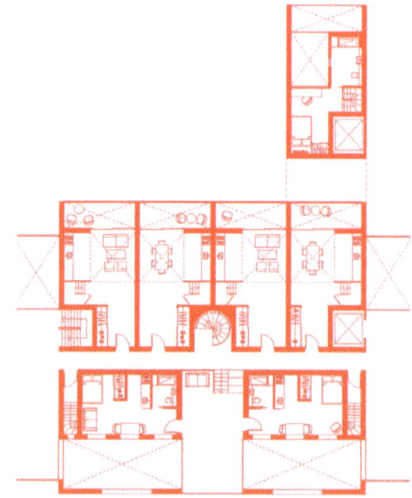

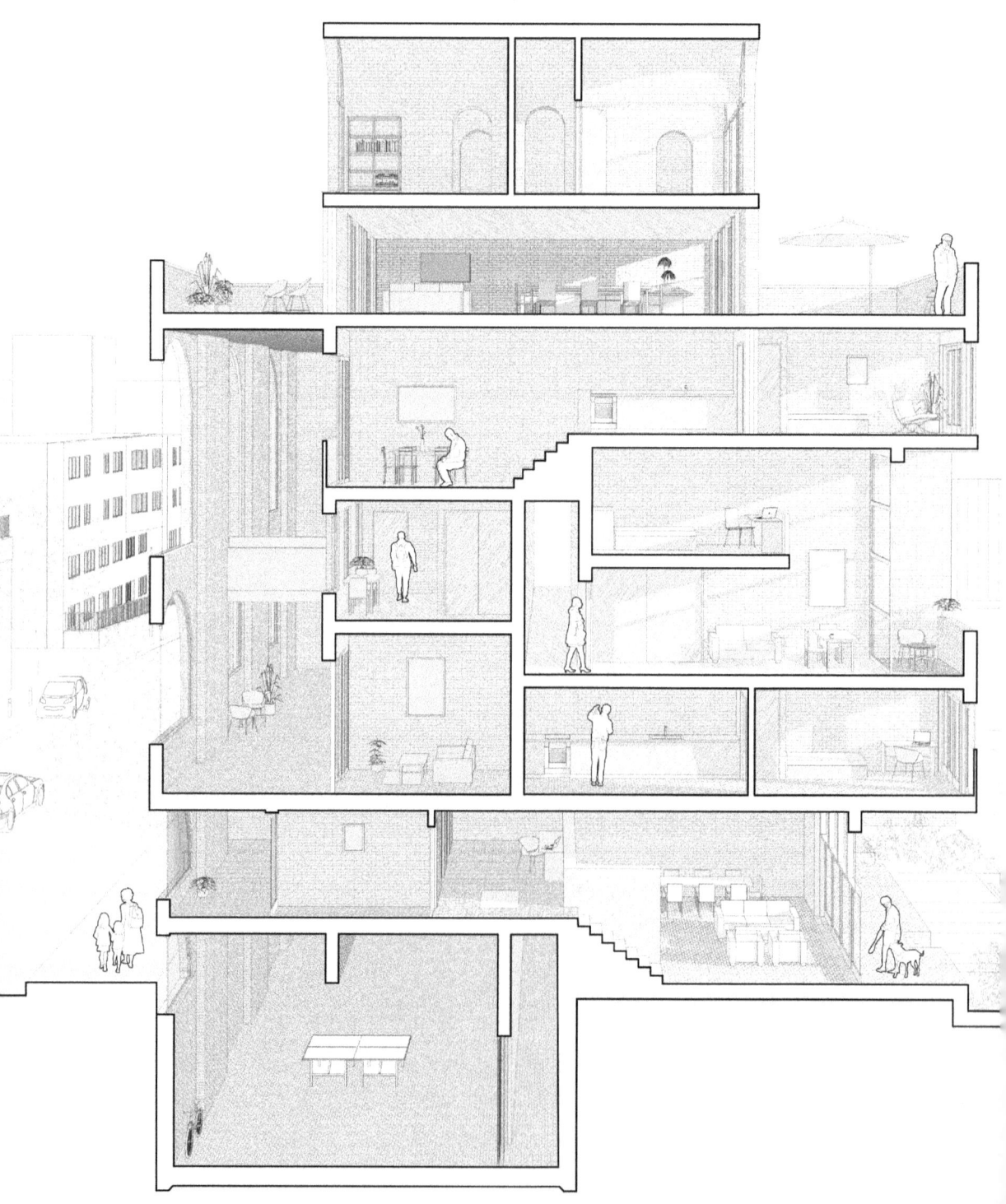

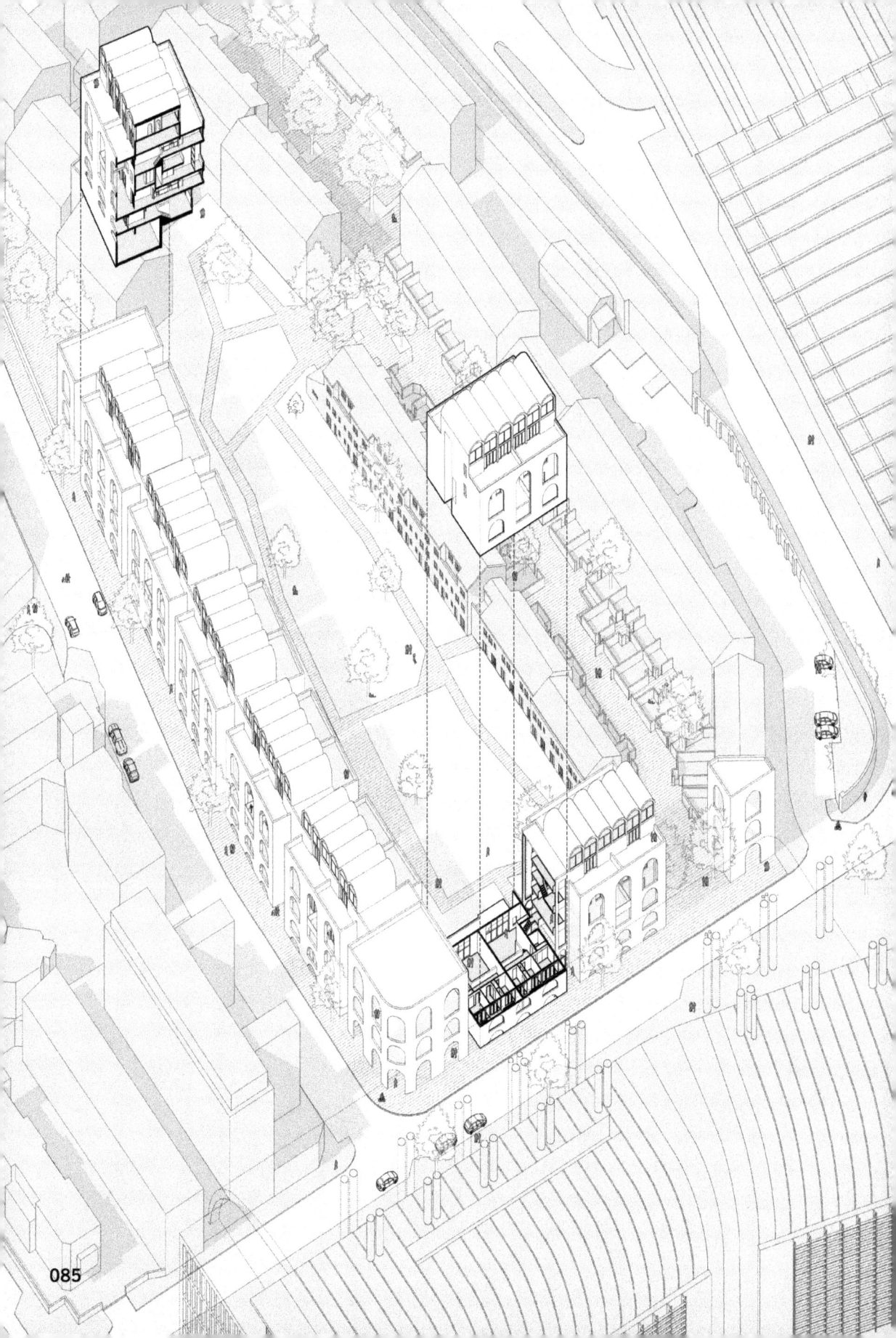

MEWS MEET LANDSCAPE

CATALINA STROE

LOCATION: SOMERS TOWN, LONDON, UK

This project combines the private intimacy of mews terraces with the public generosity of a rooftop landscape, to create a new community for growing families.

Taking inspiration from the narrow proportion, quiet atmosphere and semi-public/semi-private nature of the pebbled mews of London, the project consists of rows of two to three storey terraces laid out parallel to each other, and perpendicular to the street at a corner site in Somers Town.

Within the terraces, three types of family houses are developed around the idea of play, and organised around a central top lit staircase, with split-levels dedicated to adults entertaining and children playing independently but always with a visual connection to each other.

The spaces between each row become an ambiguous realm of simultaneously front and back yards. This is a place for welcome mats, parasols, benches, potted plants, and children's tricycles. These cobbled lanes are bisected by a diagonal public route through the entire site. As this 'desire line' cuts through the terraces, it is flanked by shops, and community rooms along the ground floor, as well as access, by way of stairs and ramps onto the roof level of the mews terraces. The rooftops of all the terraces are connected via bridges into one single high level landscape, which is offered back to the public as a park.

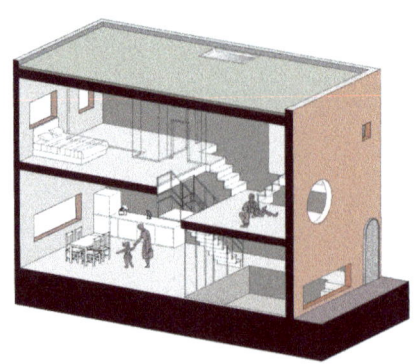

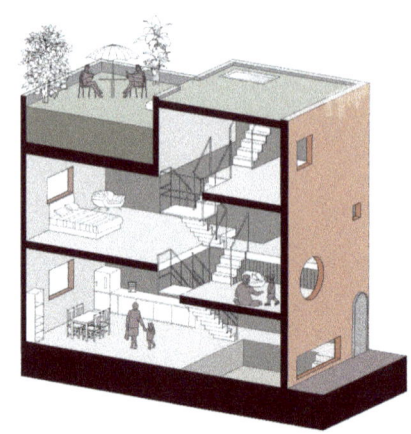

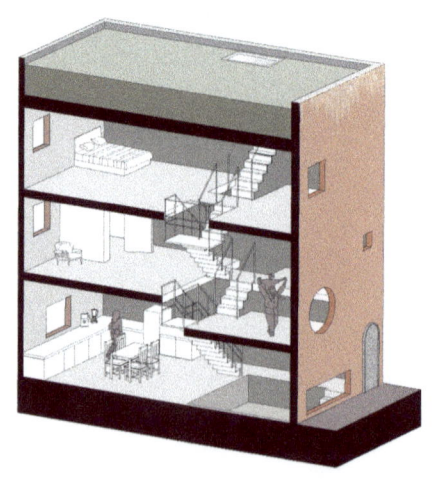

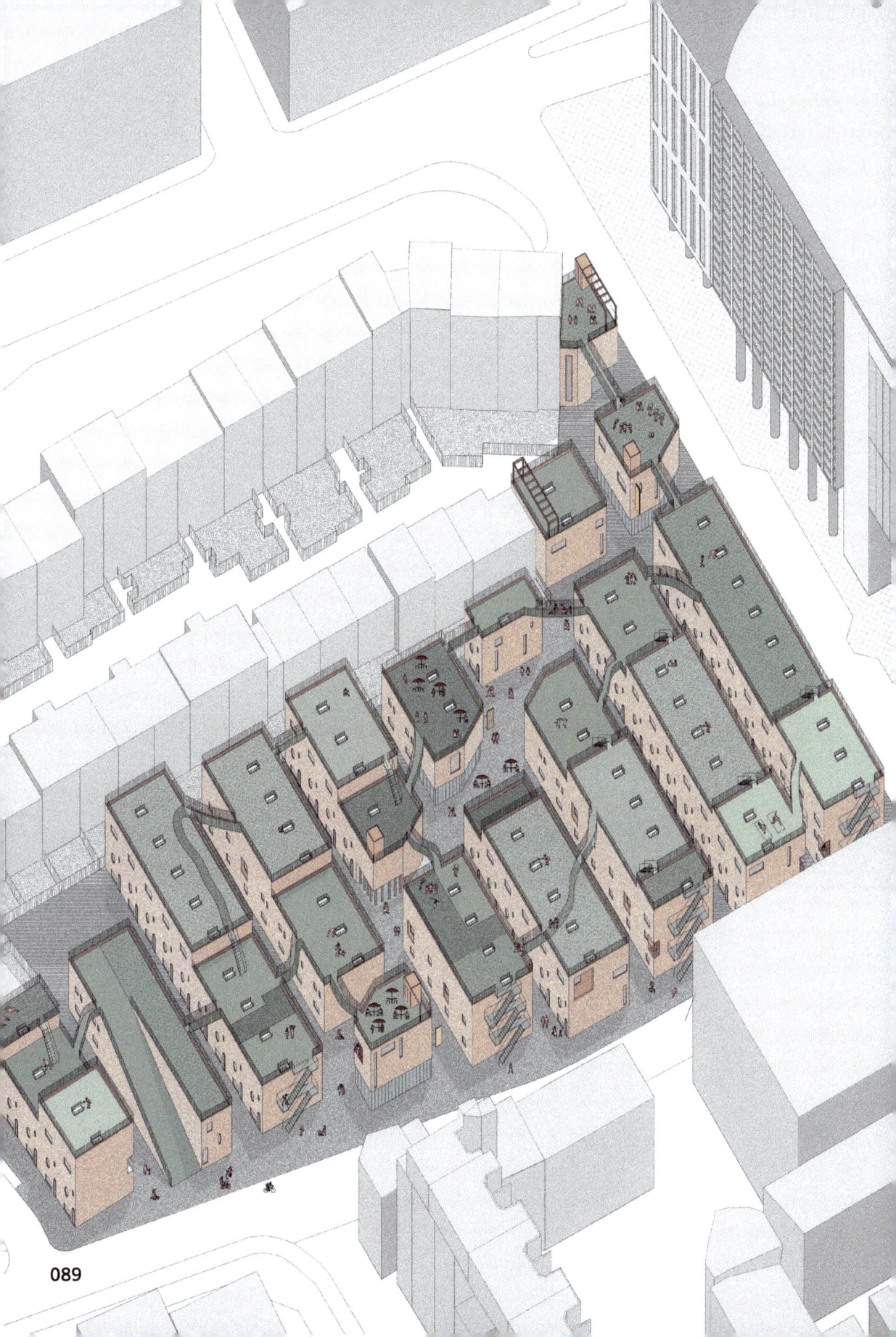

CARE IN THE COMMUNITY

LAUREN FASHOKUN

LOCATION: SOMERS TOWN, LONDON, UK

This is a multi-generational housing scheme that exploits the flexibility of the terrace house typology to accommodate changing patterns of living, and combine it with the elements of the Chinese courtyard.

The proposed terrace is a repetition of a basic cluster of three dwellings: a family home, a house for an elderly couple and a studio apartment. The three dwellings are interlocked three-dimensionally and share three separate outdoor spaces, a front yard, a courtyard, and a back yard. The front yard is where their entrances meet, the courtyard is where the family go to relax, where as the back yard becomes a play space for the children or a rear garden for the elderly. As the living needs of these inhabitants change, the families can downsize or upgrade without moving out of their neighbourhood. The studio apartment can become the home of children who are grown and want to become independent, or where carers for the elderly can rent and live.

Laid out in three bars along the site, these terraces define two key urban spaces. On one edge of the site, the terraces facing onto each other form a street which terminates in a community centre. On the other side, a back to back condition creates a playground and park which the residents can access from their back yard.

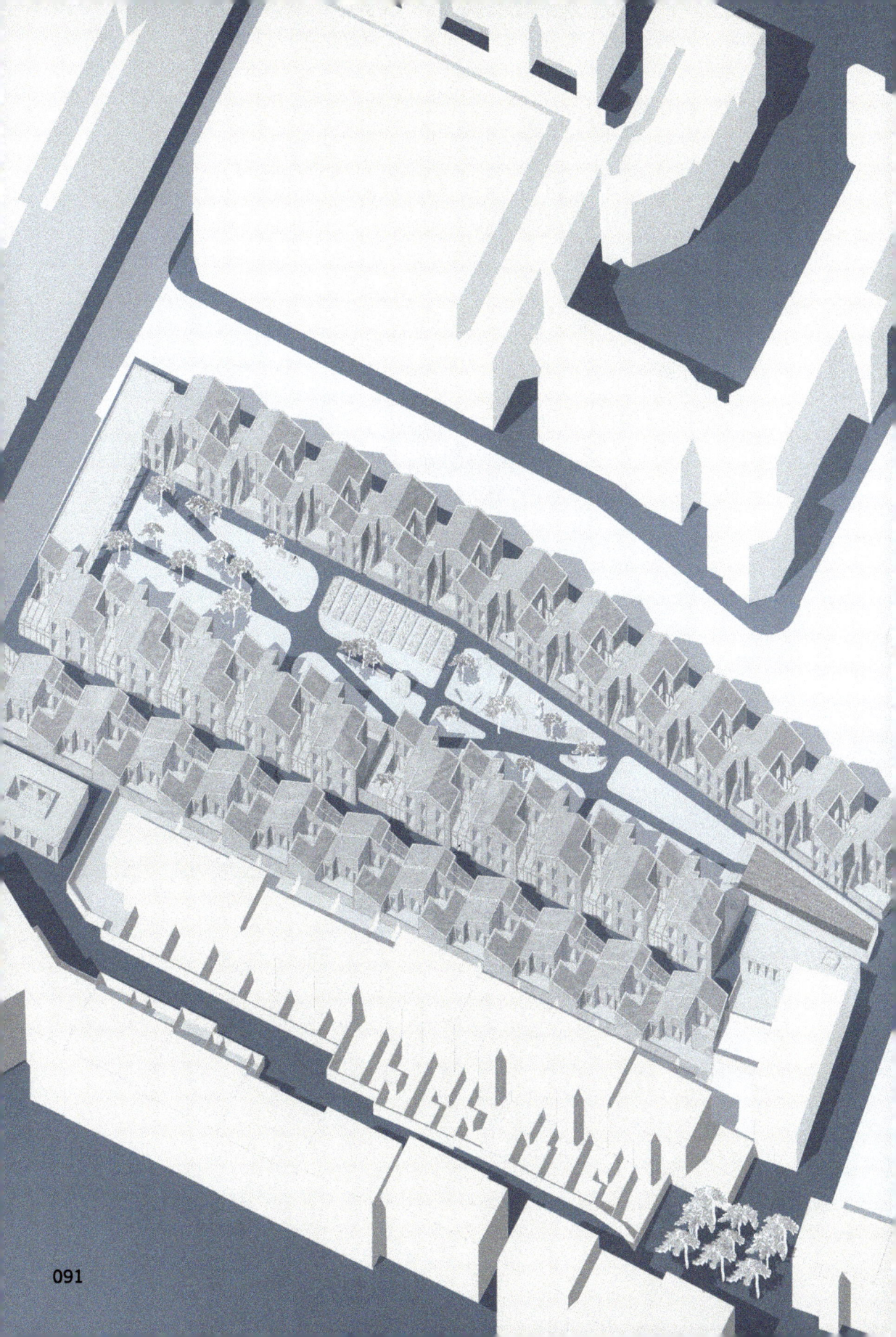

MIGRANTS WELCOME

CATALINA STROE

LOCATION: SAN YUAN LI, BEIJING, CHINA

The typology that is ubiquitous in London is put to test in Beijing in this project, which imagines an elevated terrace for migrants that hovers over the market where they work.

Conceived as a retrofit project using pre-fabricated timber structural frames and panels, the project reconfigures the interiors of a linear market in San Yuan Li in Beijing, connecting each stall within the market to a cluster of three apartments for the migrants working in the market, who are in desperate need of adequate live/work spaces to suit their round the clock presence in the market. A pair of interlocked small apartments sit immediately over the market, designed for a single market vendor or a young couple who might both be working at the market. A further storey up is a duplex family apartment, designed for migrants who decide to stay and raise a family in Beijing, but who could ill-afford to move elsewhere. These terraced duplex are accessed off a single walkway, connected to the market via staircases, and over looking an existing park, which becomes the place of rest and respite for the market workers and their families.

The material language of the timber terraces are repeated within the park to create a series of pavilions serving as community spaces, accommodating libraries, games rooms and meeting rooms, where this enclave of migrants might start to interact with local Beijing residents living around the site, and become part of the neighbourhood.

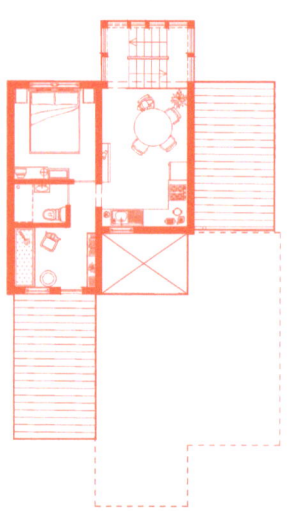
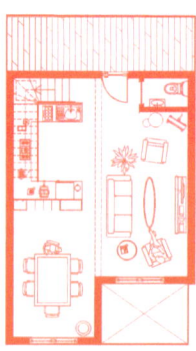

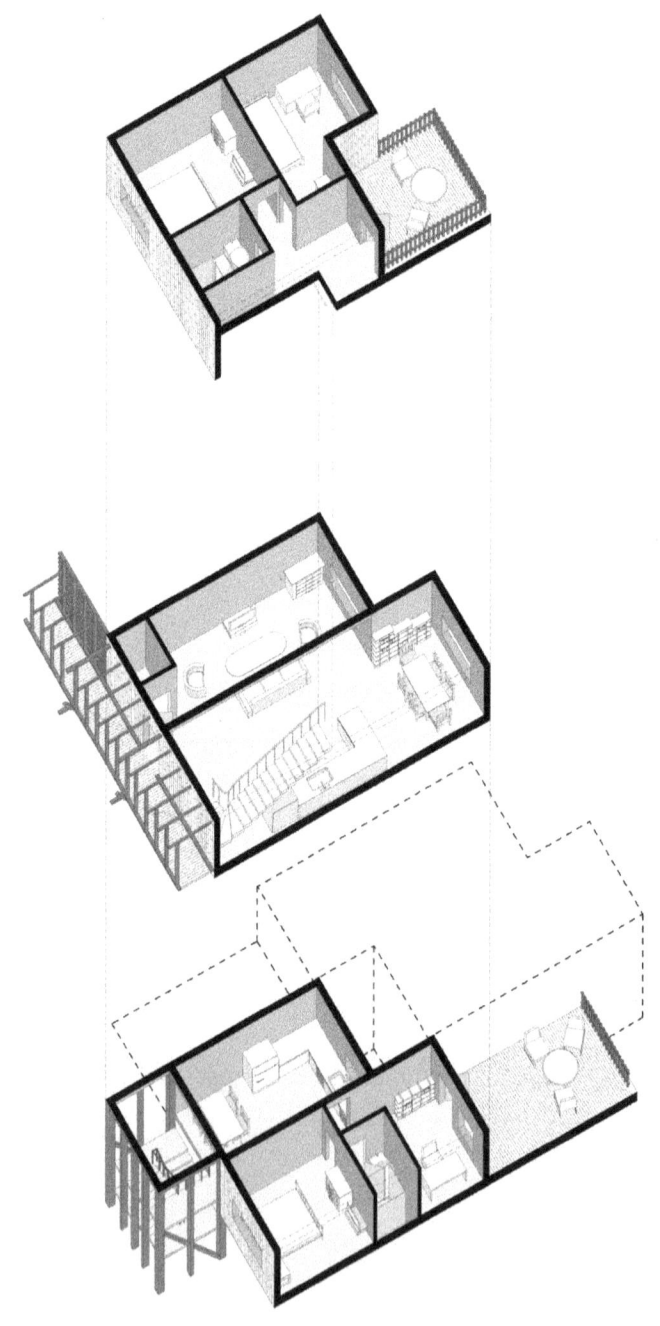

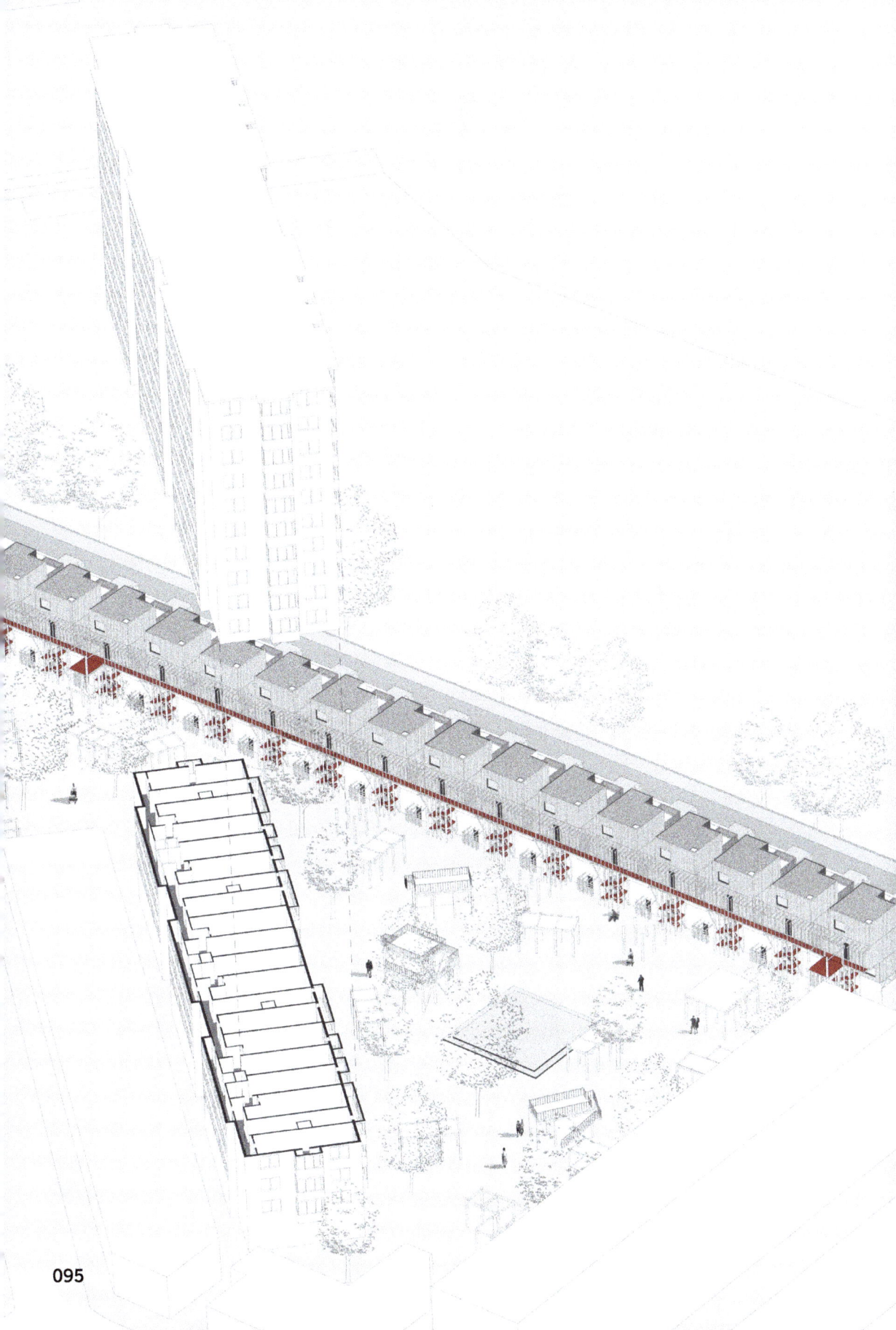

GROWING OLD TOGETHER

GABIJA GUMBEVILECIUTE

LOCATION: HOLBORN, LONDON, UK

This is a materially driven mixed tenure housing proposal that challenges the convention of front and back that defines the terrace typology.

By de-constructing the deep and narrow plan of the traditional terrace house footprint, the proposal creates a composition of four rammed earth volumes, separated by two gardens and an internal street that bisects them. This complex juxtaposition effectively creates two street frontages and means of access. This tectonic flexibility creates the condition for four types of dwellings to be created: a duo of student dorms that share a study room, two pairs of key worker overnight stay duplex studios, an elderly apartments and two family homes who share a garden. The flexibility of the design allows for one of the family homes to be internally connected to the elderly apartment, in the case of a multi-generational family taking occupation. Each dwelling is given a street address, with the key worker overnight accommodation facing the busier existing public pavement, and the other family oriented dwellings lining the quieter street created by the project's novel tectonic.

As one walk down this intimately proportioned street, the richness and solidity of the rammed earth material is rhythmically interrupted by the shared gardens and the glazed dining rooms of the family apartments overhead, offering glimpses of a shared communal life.

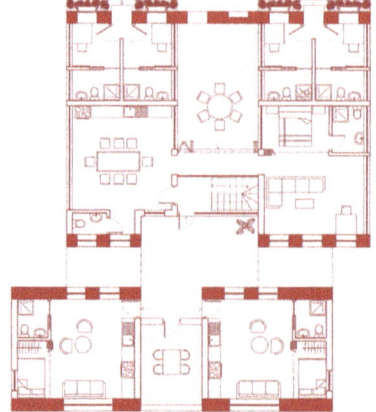
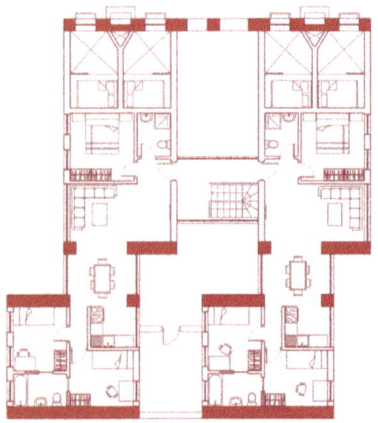

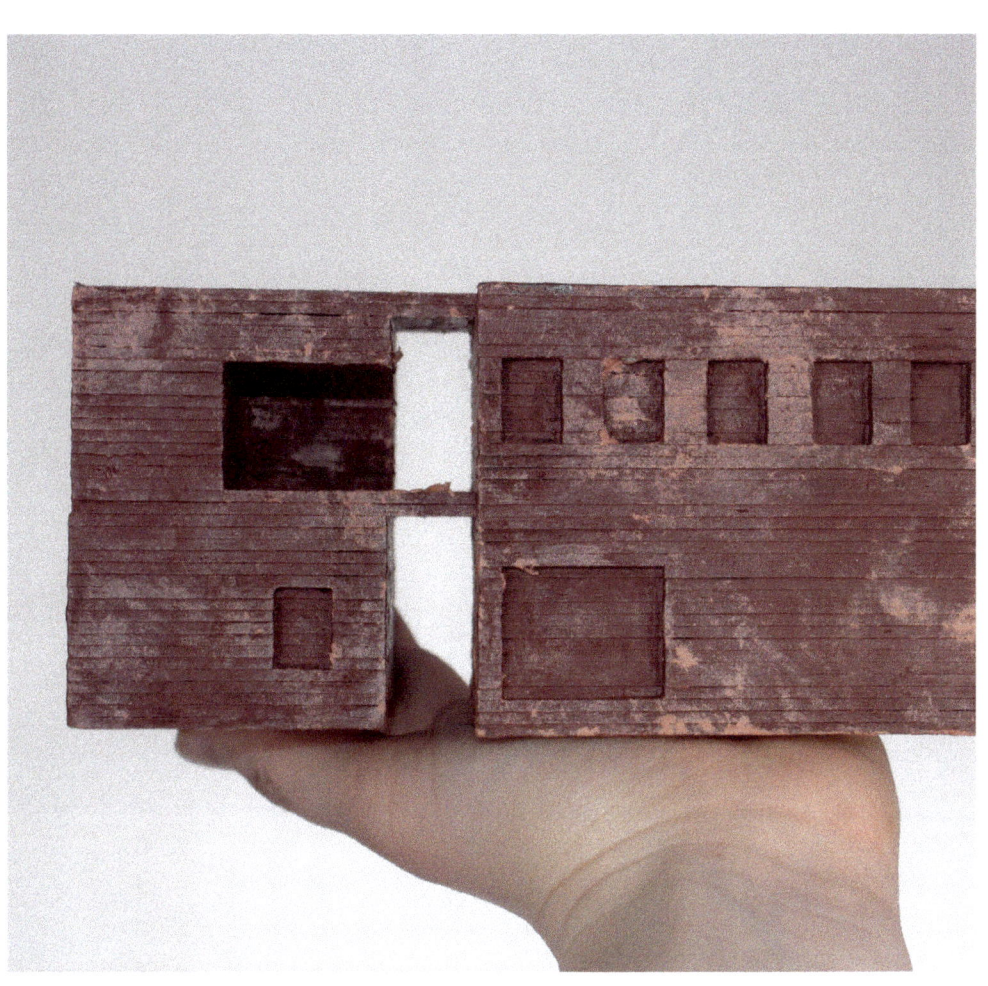

STREET LIFE

ANNA TABACU

LOCATION: NEW CROSS, LONDON, UK

This project takes inspirations from the works of Neave Brown at Fleet Road and the intimacy of the Hutongs in Beijing.

In response to the lack of a cohesive urban pattern in this part of New Cross, the project seeks to re-establish street frontages that have been lost over the decades since the destruction of the traditional terraces from WWII bombings.

Five 'streets' are created from the placement of four terraces parallel to each other, in two pairs. Each of the two pairs of terraces creates three different conditions of frontages: a public facing street, an internal alley, and a garden wall. On the ground floor, the plan reveals a series of student incubator units and homeless shelters that open onto the street. The intimate alley is flanked by entrance doors to two storey family houses that share a dining and activity space on the first floor, which bridges over the alley, providing cover over the porches. Between the two pairs of terraces is a community garden, of lush lawns and mature trees, overlooked on either side by the bedrooms of the family homes, from where access to the garden is provided via a rhythmic series of verandas and steps. The roof terrace is also accessible to the community and contains four larger family homes. The result is a mixed community where each household enjoys their own privacy whilst maintaining constant contact with their neighbours through a series of shared thoroughfares and destinations.

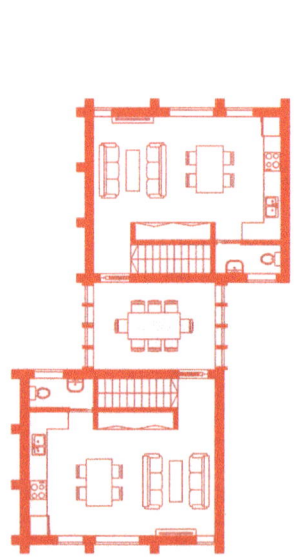
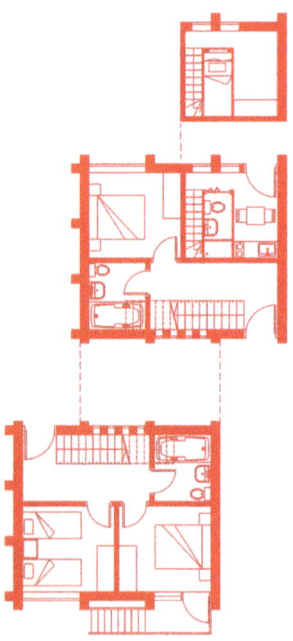

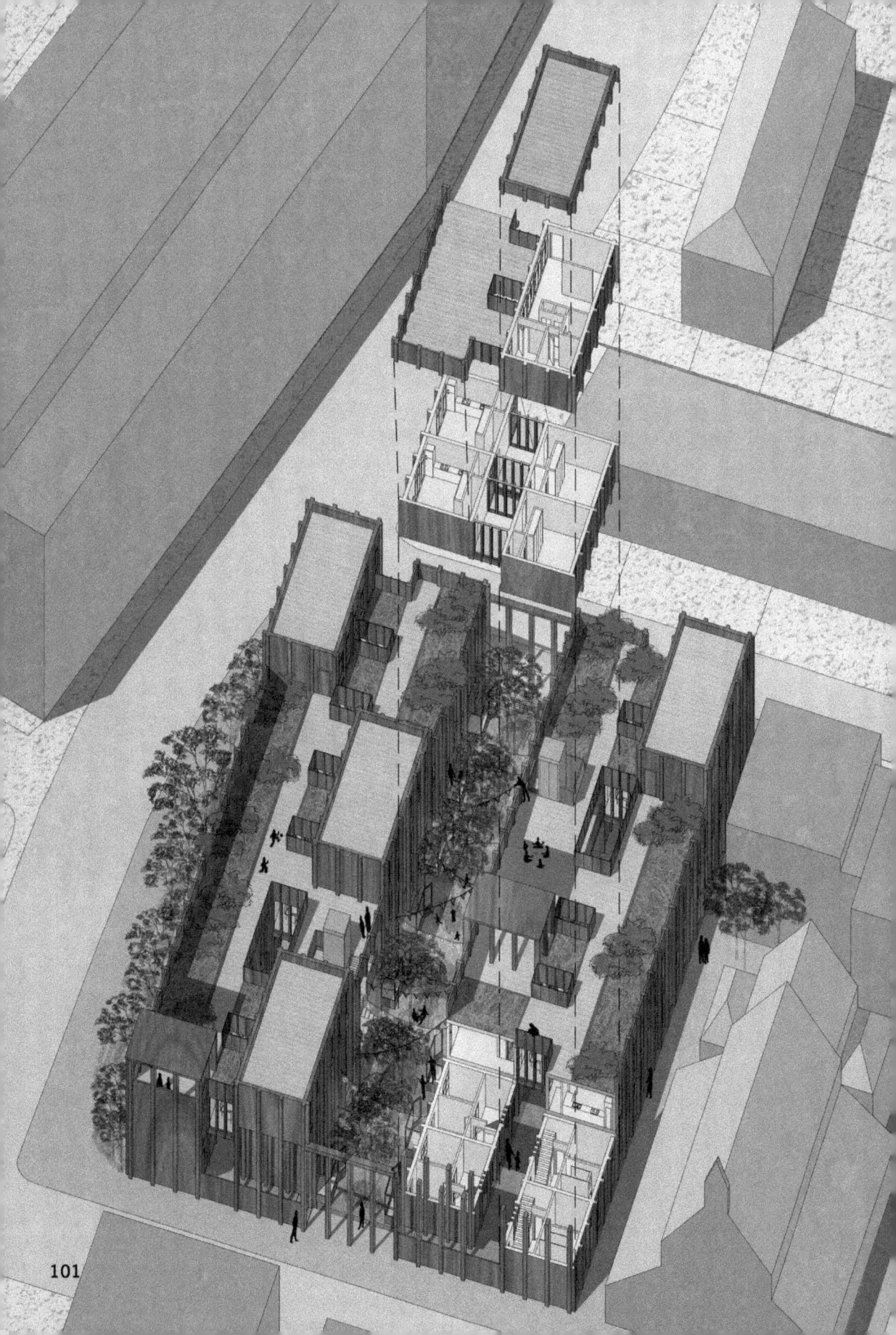

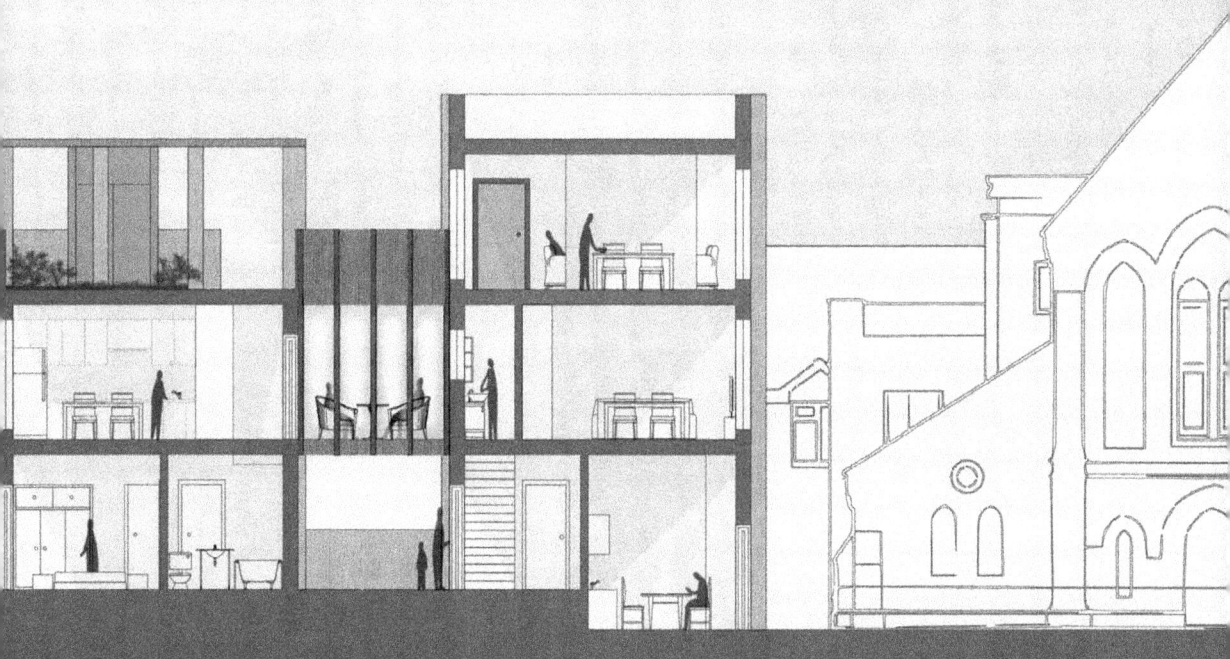

SCHOLARS' GARDEN

POONAM ALE

LOCATION: SOMERS TOWN, LONDON, UK

Located on a site adjacent to the Francis Crick Institute, this housing proposal for visiting research academics hybridises the terrace house with the collegiate quadrangle typology, in order to redefine the meaning of a contemporary scholarly life.

Whereas Oxbridge quadrangles are courtyard spaces surrounded by tectonically uniform blocks of accommodation, this project imagines a scholarly garden being enveloped by highly articulated terrace houses with a strong presence onto the street, and a strong sense of front and back. Each house is composed of three separate three scholar apartments, interlocked with each other, within a cubic volume that has been carefully carved away to form front yards, roof terraces and balconies. Within each house, the proportion of front yard facing onto the street is echoed by the shared study room facing onto a rear communal garden. Within this scholarly garden, are a meeting room and a bar. Whereas the individual study rooms within each house allow the scholars to interact with their house mates, these leisure spaces within the garden allow all the community of scholars to come together. As these terrace houses twist and turn, the site is carved into two re-interpreted quadrangles, with a street in between that diagonally bisect the site, offering views into the scholar garden and connecting the site to the wider neighbourhood. The corners of these terraces are cafes where scholarly life and public life begin to infuse.

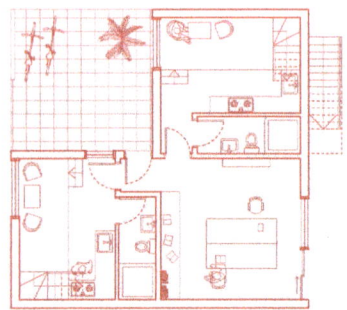 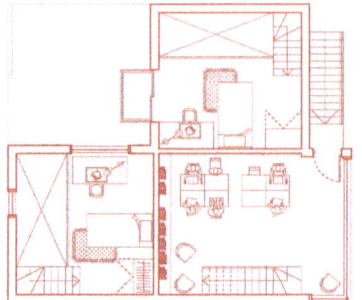 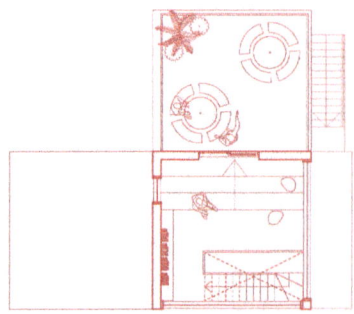

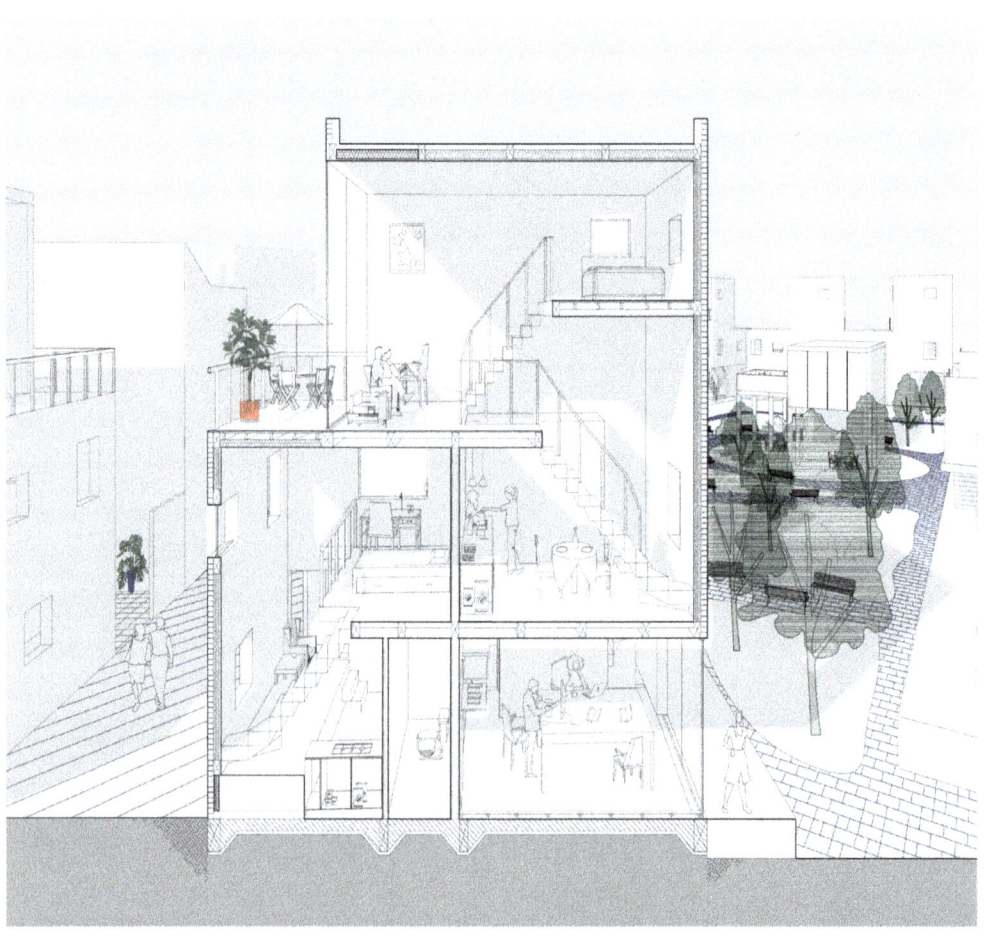

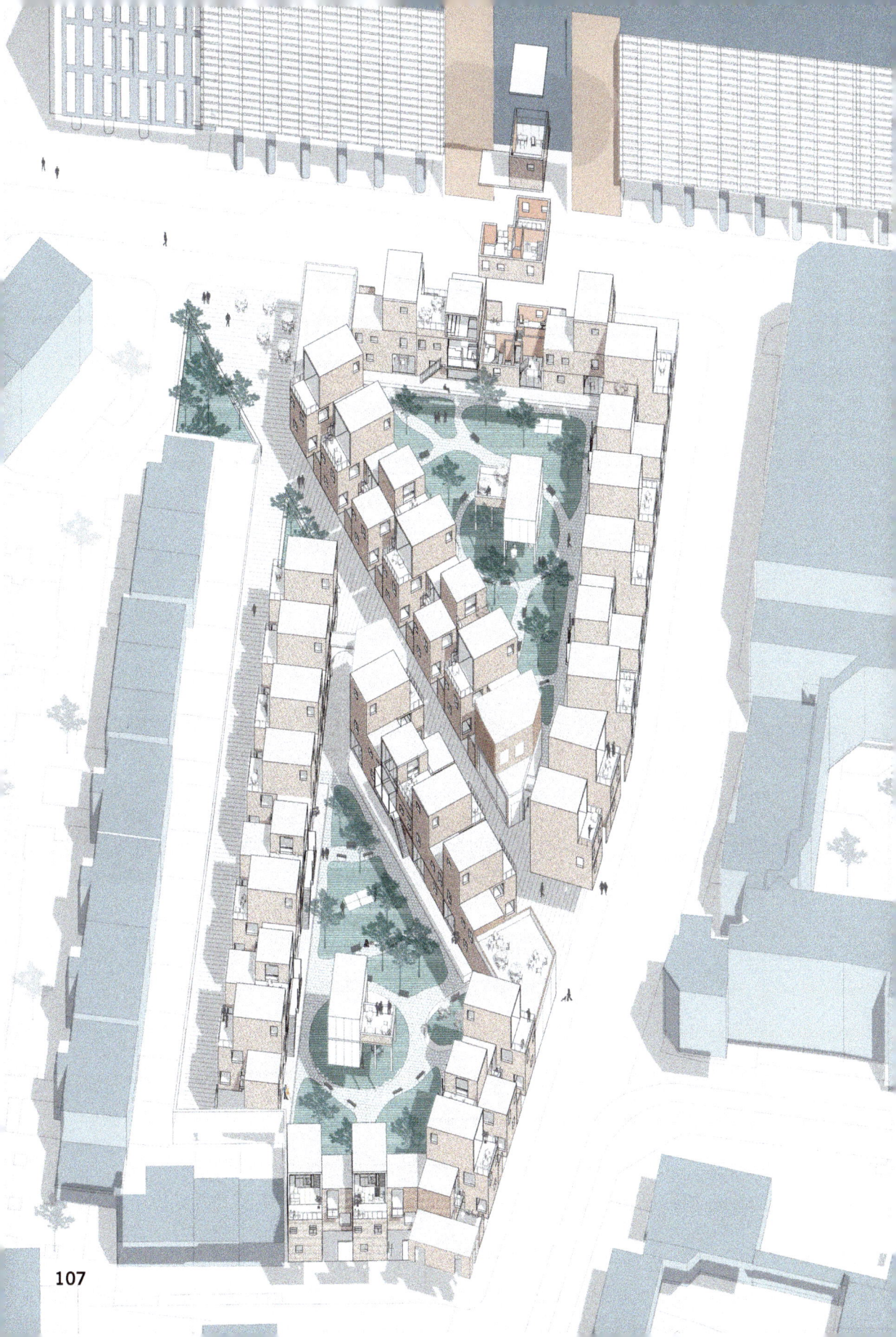

HALF WAY HOUSE

DREW YATES

LOCATION: HOLBORN, LONDON, UK

This project explores how ideas from the Georgian terraced square can combine with sustainable and prefabricated open-building systems to meet contemporary housing needs.

The fundamental feature of the proposal is a 'unfinished' terrace type. Constructed rapidly on site from prefabricated cross laminated timber panels, a series of slender three storey family houses are placed in a row with a gap of the same width between each two houses. The modular proportion of this gap means that it can be in-filled by the residents to various extent in a phased manner, to serve different private and communal needs. It may remain a garden of respite for some, but others could infill it to various extent using the same cost-effective building system to create shops, community garden sheds, meeting rooms, or simply an extra bedroom as their family grows. This terrace typology is deployed over a poorly used public realm and vacant street edge within an existing council estate in London.

The proposal includes two rows of such terrace housing that, in combination with the existing buildings, creates two new street frontages and a shared garden square. In an inversion of the Georgian model, the terraces do not have a defined front or back. Rather, the houses can be accessed from both sides, where the private space is to be found in the adaptive gap in between each house.

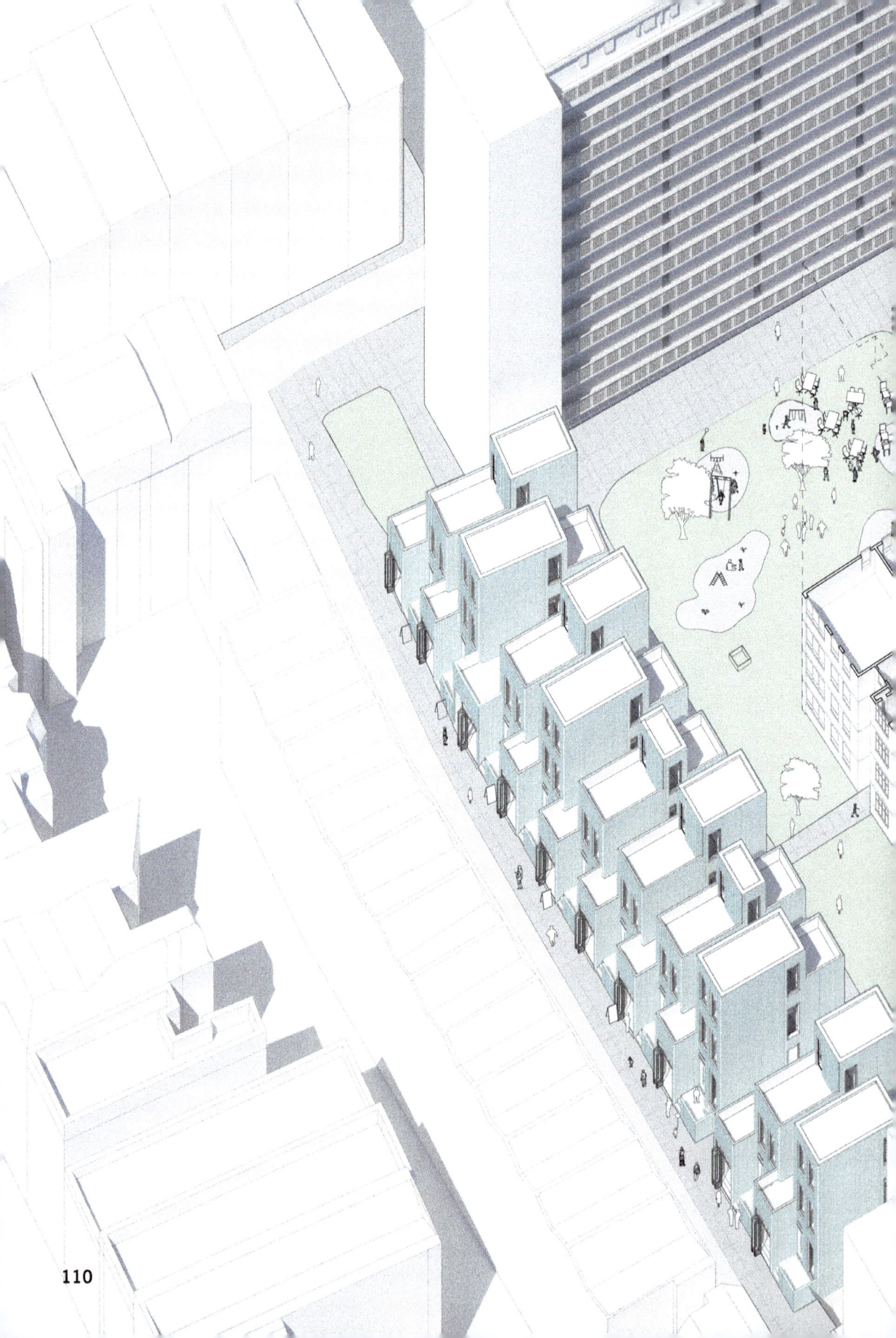

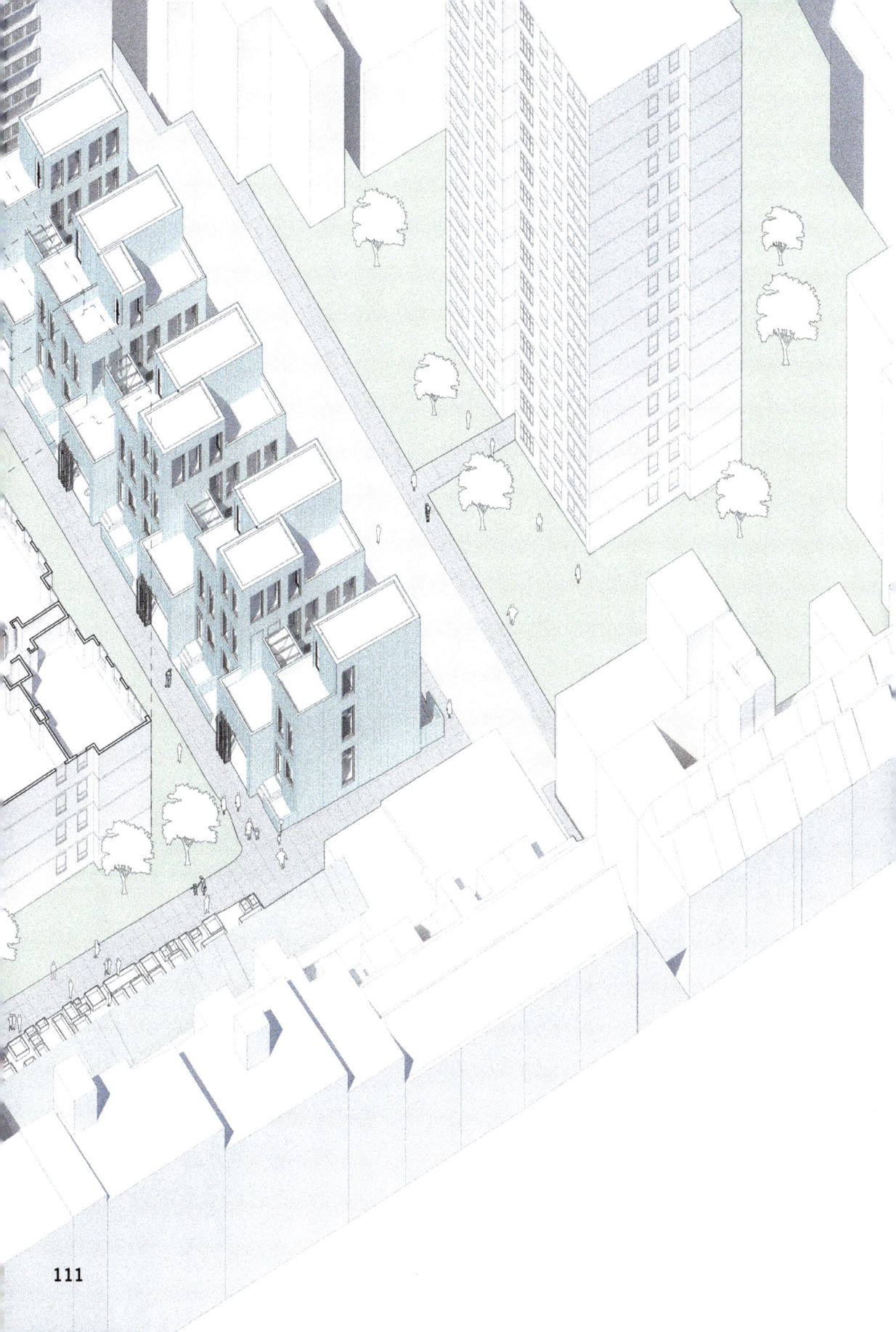

SHIKUMEN OF LONDON

LUCY BAMBURY

LOCATION: NEW CROSS, LONDON, UK

This project takes two well established housing types, the London Terrace, and the Shanghai Shikumen, and asks if they can be hybridised to provide a novel housing typology that address issues of density and context.

By turning the London terrace 90 degrees and combining it with the entry sequence of the Shanghai Shikumens, a lateral housing type is created that maintains outdoor spaces through a front courtyard and a roof terrace. This arrangement of interiors and exteriors allow the house to be stacked back to back at a higher density without compromising on privacy or outdoor amenity.

This prototype is then tested in a site in Lewisham slated for social housing redevelopment. In addition to providing family houses in a borough where the majority of new housing created is in the form of apartments, it also combats a lack of street frontage in the neighbourhood by creating a series of parallel streets activated by courtyards.

The front entrance courtyard becomes an outdoor room of sort, providing an ante-space upon entering the private realm. As one moves from living space on the ground floor up to the sleeping spaces on the first and second floor, the staircase contains extra-deep half landings that almost becomes rooms in themselves, allowing the inhabitant to enjoy small but intensely rewarding private moments of joy as they ascend the building.

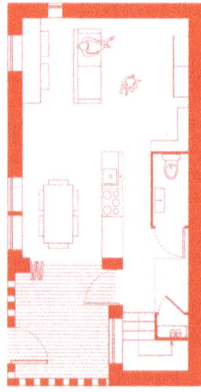
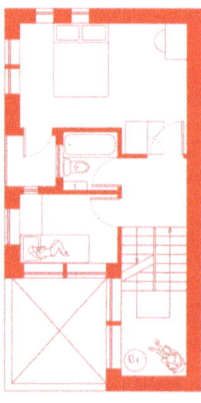
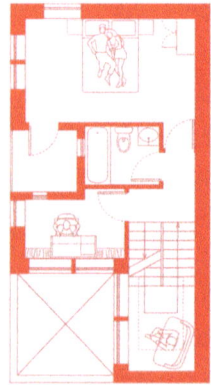

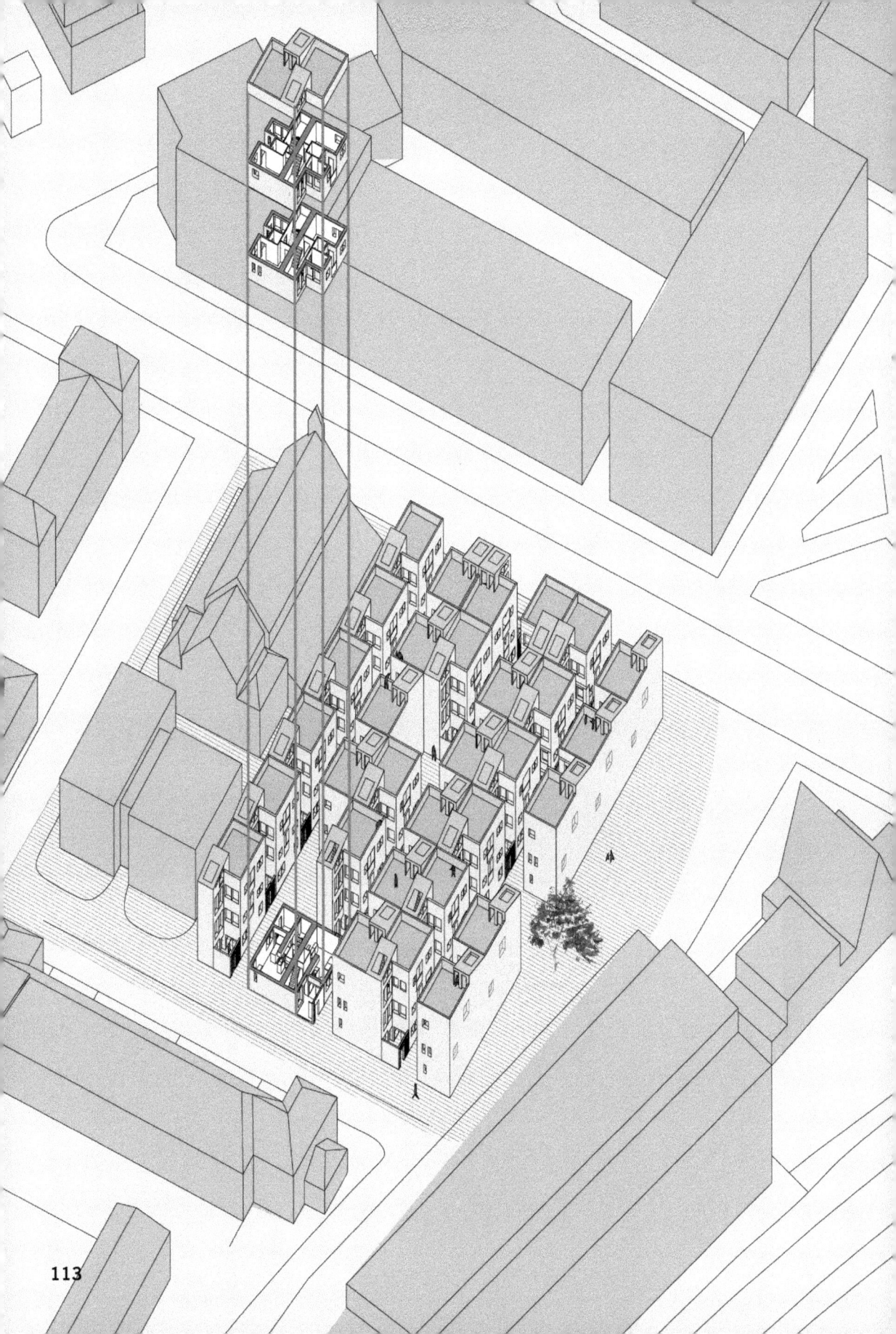

ON ENCLAVES AND THRESHOLDS

KEREN HE, DAVID PORTER, JOHN ZHANG

JZ: David mentioned the idea of 'enclaves' in discussing some of the social issues relating to post-war modernist housing experiments in London. This is a very interesting term. Very often, the sites we look at in Beijing and London are thought of as enclaves. I wonder if we could explore this terminology further and why we gravitate towards it. Keren, are you able to elucidate this, particularly the relevance of 'enclaves' in Beijing's urban morphology? David, how do you think 'enclaves' are defined differently European cities, and what wider differences within architectural culture does this reflect?

KH: We developed the enclave/exclave concept as the main scheme of the studio. Beijing today is a city whose forms are seemingly based on a series of nested enclaves, which cover a variety of geographic and spatial places. Enclaves or exclaves could refer to a variety of places—the city slum (usually equivalent to the Chinese term, "city villages"); the transformed mixed-ownership courtyard complex in the old town; the ignored areas in-between clearly defined, fenced real-estate properties; municipal infrastructure (roads, highway, greenbelt, etc.) "cutting" in the neighbourhood, or even those fashionable, expensive new building complexes "inserted" into a traditional neighbourhood. In the aforementioned cases, the boundaries around the enclaves are not always clear; the thresholds between public and private spaces are undefined or altered in order to accommodate different situations and many public spaces serve functions that deviate from the original intention of their design. These issues constitute the Studio's primary focus. The purpose of this studio is not merely to investigate the physical enclaves, but to explore the interactions between enclave/exclave spaces and their surroundings within an urban context. What were the spatial features before? Where are the boundaries? What spatial, psychological, social, or cultural changes occurred along the boundaries after implanting an enclave? What role does "gentrification" play? Questions such as these were raised and discussed during our investigations, informed by the diverse perspectives of our cross-cultural teams.

DP: Viewed from a European perspective, 'enclave' is a very problematic term, for it describes places that are separate from the body of the city, areas from which part of the population are excluded, districts that are 'no-go areas', where some are allowed to enter, or feel comfortable to enter, but others are excluded. For this reason, 'enclaves' are considered to be undesirable. This may be a growing European reality, but it is not the European ideal. We talk of 'neighbourhoods' rather

A typical Hutong neighbourhood enclave near Baitasi, Beijing

than 'enclaves'.

The urban forms of most European cities have been shaped by incremental and accumulative changes dating back to when they became industrialised in the 19th century. In London, under the pattern of modern city streets lies a rural pattern of fields and villages, where each village had a church, a market, some shops and, as the 19th century progressed, a school. London grew quickly as the industrial revolution progressed with the old villages finding themselves linked together into a city, but each one, for keen observers, retained a recognisable identity, now described as a neighbourhood. Importantly, these neighbourhood districts have no boundary wall and so a pedestrian can walk from one to another without difficulty, and from one recognisable neighbourhood to another across the whole city. The city is one loose network, sometimes regular, sometimes irregular, like a giant spider's web.

As such, the term 'neighbourhood' is more commonly used than 'enclave' although it has no clear-cut definition. This term neighbourhood (sometimes 'district') rose to prominence in the years after the second world war when the leadership of the modern movement was passed by Le Corbusier to a younger generation in preparation for the 10th Congress of CIAM. The group that prepared the congress called themselves 'Team 10'. They radically reset the urban agenda by rejecting the whole-sale demolition of the older cities and their replacement by the city of towers. They were interested in 'patterns of association' and 'identity'. They believed in retaining the historic core of cities and studied the life of the streets.

This change came about for a number of reasons: partly because this younger generation had witnessed the destruction of many of Europe's finest cities in the war and so did not romanticise demolition, and partly due to a change in our understanding of how cities worked. In the 19th Century and early 20th century the critics of the poor conditions in fast growing cities in the West emphasised the physically squalid conditions of the poor whose homes were cramped, damp, and unsanitary. They identified the buildings as the problem. After the second world war and with the rise of the discipline of sociology, the picture of modern urban life in the West was viewed a little differently. Although what the sociologists found was often still cramped, damp and insanitary, they did something new and looked beyond the buildings and talked to the residents! They often reported a strong sense of belonging, and of neighbourliness. These parts of the cities were not all bad! There were good aspects of the social patterns supported by old pattern of inhabitation. The further change of perspective came when the results of the first wave of post-war rebuilding had been completed. It was found that, although the improved physical conditions (bathrooms and kitchens for example) were much appreciated, there was also a marked sense of loss, a loss of the sense of being part of a 'neighbourhood'. Although it took a long time to change the policies of government, for progressive architects the question of urban form had been transformed.

In China, on the other hand, the pattern of neighbourhoods in cities like Beijing is radically different. Industrialisation and urbanisation have

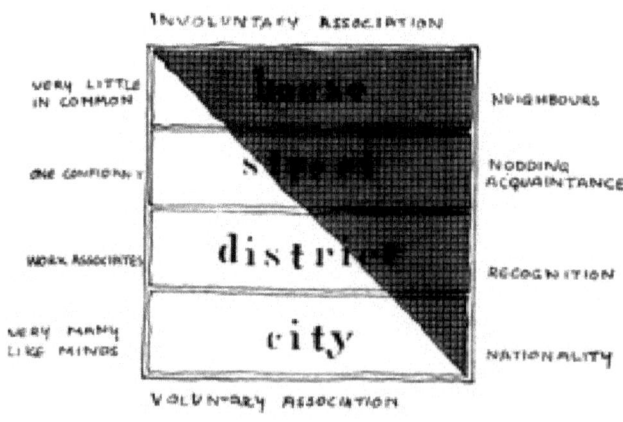

Alison Smithson's diagram of involuntary/voluntary association, 1951

The residential enclave adjacent to CAFA seen from the architecture school building at CAFA

occurred with dramatic speed over the last third of the 20th Century and into the first quarter of the 21st. The old parts of the city, like Beijing's Forbidden City and the hutongs that surround it, are very old. While the new is very new. The pattern of incremental adjustment over time that is the story of the European City is absent and there is an almost complete separation of the past from the present, with little interaction between the two.

This separation can be called the 'enclave': a district separated from its surroundings. For example, the CAFA campus is across the road from the district of Huajiadi. CAFA looks across a road at Huajiadi, and it looks back. But they are different worlds. Huajiadi comprises 5-storey slabs, built in the 1980s, to house workers coming into Beijing, many from rural areas, so this was their first experience of urban life. The Huajiadi enclave has a school, a nursery, a community centre but is a walled and gated community. You can walk within it but not easily cross it. It does not legibly link to the 'neighbouring' enclaves.

The CAFA enclave, built over the last 30 years, is also walled and gated with everything needed for a modern campus. Beyond is a park, but the park, like the campus, is walled and gated, and so while you can see the park from the campus and the campus from the park, you can not walk between them – you have to leave the campus-enclave, and circulate on the main road system, then re-enter the park-enclave that sits next door to CAFA. Modern Beijing lacks the porosity of European cities and so is more friendly to cars than to pedestrians and cyclists.

JZ: These two different perspectives that you have provided precisely demonstrate the need for an interrogation of comparative urban morphology. The same terminology takes on rather different meanings between Beijing and London. I guess the 'enclave' as described by its physical property is much more identifiable in Beijing than London, we see it in the traditional Siheyuans courtyards, the socialist 'Danwei' (work unit) compounds, and the ubiquitous gated real estate communities, or 'Xiaoqu'. It seems that living in enclaves in China is a much more normalised condition. When we speak of enclave in places like London, we think of communities that are not just physically separated from the city, but sometimes socially and economically excluded from the rest of society, and so the architecture of these enclaves has come to represent their problems. The urgency in the West seems to always revolve around how we can break down enclaves and connect them to the city. However, in China, I think it is often the very separation from the city that allows for enclaves to develop a degree of autonomy that protects the community it accommodates, a kind of resistance to prevailing model of urban expansion and regeneration which may threaten the future of a particular group of people in the city. One thinks of the urban villages and artist collectives in Beijing and the enclave they have come to identify with.

These differences provide a rich and fertile ground for students to reassess their understandings of community and their architectural relationship to the city. It makes things less black and white; it forces them to lose their prejudice and look at things afresh.

JZ: Over the years, the studio has developed a particular approach to understanding residential enclave sites through personal mappings of thresholds and spaces of transition, between the home and the city, between the private and the public. Keren, would you be able to explicate the rationale behind this approach? David, in what way is this investigation into threshold constitutes a mean to understand differences in architectural culture between China and the West?

KH: As Stan Allen said, "The problem of architecture and the contemporary city is also in part a problem of representation." [01] In China, the historic cities like Beijing that were constructed by collective memory within finite, physical boundaries have long been transformed. In response to this change, conventional static architectural presentation has to give way to more complex, dynamic, and interdisciplinary methods. Kevin Lynch's phenomenological approach to studying the legibility of the city provides a useful guide for our study. In our studio, it is also very beneficial that the variety of cultural background from faculty and students provide interesting and various reflections on urban issues. Each team of students are from various cultural backgrounds. They are asked to look into a neighbourhood together: observing, recording, questioning, and participating in community activities. During the process, teachers and students learn from each other—not only academic knowledge and techniques, but cultural values and personal styles as well. These are invaluable experiences for everyone involved.

DP: Each culture has an idea of 'dwelling' and an idea of 'neighbourhood' but beyond that, there is no precise, universal definition. Each student when considering these words, are really thinking "I know what this means for me", but it does not mean that there is any

Beijing threshold study by Zuzanna Osiecka (JID Studio 2017 Alumni)

Facing towards and away from the light/view outside, a cultural practice?

clear-cut shared definition. This problem of establishing a shared set of understandings led us to look more closely at the thresholds that define the dwelling and hence its relationships to neighbourhood and the city beyond. We could all agree what we meant by "window", "door" and "gateway" and go around Beijing and observe them in use. Indeed, doors and windows are manufactured in the same way internationally, and can be selected from identical product catalogues. Thresholds are basic architectural elements that are identifiable and tangible. In the end, the intelligent distribution of such elements constitutes much of what we all call architectural design. This is not a glamorous way of looking at architecture, but I think it is both true and universal, that is, buildings in China and in Europe have these elements. But in each culture, they have a different meanings.

As simple examples, we were struck by a significant cultural difference between the European students and their CAFA colleagues. On settling into the studio, the European students often sought a desk in front of the window. By contrast the CAFA students did not seek this intimate relationship with a window at all. They would seek places away from the window and made sure that there was a blind (preferably pulled down) and an array of plants and other objects to screen them from the view. So, windows are pretty much the same everywhere but the cultural role they play in what we later came to call the 'poetics of habitation' is often very different. Beijing windows, in new buildings as well as old ones, act as a kind of protective filter between the room behind and the neighbourhood and city beyond, in a culture where sunlight is not traditionally enjoyed directly.

Despite this evidence, I found it really strange that in crits students would say what they seem to say all around the world: "I placed my window here to establish a visual connection". Chinese students would then design apartments with wall to wall and floor to ceiling glazing. From this I learned that in China, just like at home, students are more comfortable looking for ideas surfing the internet than they are walking around and using their eyes, particularly using their eyes to ask questions. The world in front of them seems to hold little interest or creative potential.

The ambition of the studio is that each student, whether Chinese or European, will gain an understanding that there is no fixed model of what a dwelling, a neighbourhood, or a city might be. They will remember their experience here and remember that, whatever they may be, they could also be otherwise.

JZ: To follow up on David's example, one of the most fascinating things in this studio is to see how students from the UK make observations on things that their Chinese counterparts take for granted, and vice versa. For example, the cages around balconies on Chinese residential blocks proved a frequent source of fascination for foreign students when they first arrive in Beijing: why are they there, what else does it do apart from providing security, how does it change the view into and out of the apartment, how similar is this feature to traditional screening elements, etc. As the questions about this seemingly common phenomenon becomes more incisive, one begins to re-examine aspects of Chinese spatial sensibility and how they are manifested in the contemporary every day. It is precisely the goal of the studio to overcome this self-imposed blindness through mutual engagement with the 'foreign other'. When fresh eyes are applied to what we think we have in common and what we think we know well, new insights often present themselves. However, old habits die hard, all too often the students default to what they considered to be unquestionable received wisdoms. So more than exposing the cultural differences, the most valuable outcome of the study into thresholds, is that it simply opens up a range of new possibilities for students, to acknowledge that there is more than one way of doing things.

Notes

(01) Stan Allen, "Mapping the unmappable, on Notation" in *Practice: Architecture, Technique, and Representation.* Amsterdam, Marston, 2000. p.36

Urban Village enclave studies by Chloe Lambermont, part of the 2015-2016 international studio cohort at CAFA

The entrance threshold to Wu Liangyong's Ju'er Hutong housing

EAST MEETS WEST

JOHN ZHANG

RE-TRACING THE HISTORY OF ENCOUNTER BETWEEN FOREIGN AND CHINESE ARCHITECTS

The conversation around the exchange between China and the West within the realm of architecture is typically focused on the role played by foreign architects in the dramatic transformation of the Chinese built environment in recent decades. However, this contemporary narrative (since 1978) of exchange and influence between China and the West is not historically unique. Despite distinctively different political, economic, cultural, and social historical contexts, Chinese architecture has been engaged in a dialogue with the West for well over 200 years. Critically, the presence of this foreign influence, whilst persistence, is not contiguous, but rather cyclical in nature.

Gardens, pagodas and perspectives

The wider context of East West exchange can be traced back to as early as the Han Dynasty in the 3rd Century BC, when the Silk Road was established, which linked China to Hellenic Greece and subsequently the Roman Empire. The exotic stories brought back from China by Marco Polo in the 13th Century AD, and the world map drew up by Matteo Ricci for the Ming Emperor Wanli in the 17th Century are evidence of this continuous cultural dialogue between East and West.

It is fascinating to note that for a large period of history, the flow of influence was as much from East to West as it is the other way round. Indeed, as far as architecture is concerned, Europeans were intrigued by the Chinese pavilions and gardens depicted on the fine porcelain tea ware imported from China. The Chinesisches Haus in Sanssouci Park in Potsdam, Germany, as well as the Chinese Pagoda by William Chambers in Kew exemplified the peculiar European (re)interpretations of Chinese architecture, or Chinoiserie. Many have argued that the development of the English Landscape Garden tradition was also influenced by ideas of the Chinese garden [01], albeit at times from distorted and fantasised accounts [02].

In so far as architecture and its stylistic expression is concerned, whilst there may not be a single moment when the flow of influence becomes dominantly West to East, the arrival of Italian jesuits Giuseppe Castiglione and Michel Benoist in the court of the Qing emperor Qianlong in the mid-18th Century does represent a critical milestone. Where Chinese artists have been depicting the three dimensional spatial depth of architecture through primarily isometric projections, Castiglione introduced perspective

Giuseppe Castiglione et al. *Qianlong Viewing a Peacock Spreading its Tail*, 1758. Colour on paper. 340 x 537cm. Palace Museum, Beijing.

projections in his paintings of buildings and interiors, which amalgamated Chinese compositional sensibility with European oil painting techniques. Architectural representation was given a new mean of visual communication. Together with Michel Benoist, Castiglione worked on the designs of buildings in the Old Summer Palace (Yuan Ming Yuan) for the Qing Emperor Qianlong in 1747, where a hybridised architectural style incorporated elements of both traditional Chinese and European baroque and rococo elements.

Masters and apprentices

The next critical phase of interaction between China and the West within the discourse of architecture spans from the 1910s to the 1940s, between the collapse of the Qing Empire and the founding of the People's Republic of China under the Chinese Communist Party.

During this period, in the foreign colonies and concessions in cities such as Beijing, Tianjin, Shanghai, and Hong Kong, foreign architects arrived to serve colonial clients, designing administrative headquarters, offices, banks, residences, and places of entertainment. Along side these were universities, factories, cinemas, and department stores: building types that simply did not exist in China prior to the start of the 20th Century. Commissions from Chinese clients and the fledgling Nationalist government soon followed.

Foreign architects such as Palmer and Turner, Laszlo Hudec, and Henry Murphy, through their built work and presence, introduced a wide variety of fin de siecle western architectural styles to China, ranging from Beaux Arts, eclecticism, neo-classicism, art deco, and early Bauhaus modernism. In places like Shanghai, buildings by individuals such as Hudec, have come to define the metropolitan identity of the city.

However, foreign influence on the discourse of Chinese architecture went beyond the mere appearance of the built environment. The first generation of Chinese architects who would define the nature of the Chinese architectural profession and pedagogy were all educated abroad. Liang Sicheng, Yang Tingbao, and Tong Jun had all studied at the University of Pennsylvania, between 1921-1925 under the tutelage of Paul Philippe Cret (1876-1945). Chen Zhanxiang was studying under Sir Patrick Abercrombie in 1938 at the University of Liverpool. Liu Dunzhen began his studies at Tokyo Institute of Technology in 1916, and would go on to establish the first Chinese private practice, Hua Hai, with Liu Shiying in 1922.

When these Chinese architects returned to China, the offices of foreign architects became their launch pad to prominence. Yang Tingbao worked in the office of Paul Cret in the United States, before joining the Chinese practice Jitai (Kwan Chu & Yang) in 1927. Lü Yanzhi worked for Henry Murphy first in his New York office, then in the Shanghai office from 1921, before setting up his own practice Zhenyu in partnership with Huang Tanpu. Zhuang Jun, another pioneering Chinese architects, had also assisted the work of Henry Murphy in Beijing before setting up his own practice in 1925.

In parallel to practice, foreign trained Chinese architects also became pivotal in the formation of the Chinese architectural education system. Liu Dunzhen and Liu Shiying established the very first department of architecture in China at the Suzhou Industrial Specialist College in 1923. Five years later in 1928, Liang Sicheng, who was trained under the Beaux Arts tradition, established the architecture department at Northeast University in Shenyang, the first formalised higher education curriculum that taught architecture following the western model.

Importantly, this engagement between China and the West was not simply one directional. As Chinese architects experimented with western modernism in China, foreign architects were simultaneously being influenced by the richness of traditional Chinese architecture. For example, Chinese American architect Lee Gum Poy designed YWCA building on the Bund in Shanghai, where explicitly Chinese vernacular architectural motifs were tested in the design of an essentially Art Deco building with a western programme.

The deep reaching interaction between foreign and Chinese architects during this period was brought to an abrupt end by the onset of the Second World War in 1937. The calamities of war made the practice of architecture in China extremely difficult for foreign and Chinese architects. Whilst the war exposed the transitory nature of their presence in China, at the end of this distinctive cycle of exchange, colonial foreign architects have facilitated the inception of the modern Chinese profession, pedagogy, and participated in early experimentations to reconcile China's architectural heritage with western modernity, the cumulative influence of which would be felt for decades to come, despite the radically different socio-political context of the ensuing decades.

Learning From Big Brother

What followed the end of the Second World War and the triumph of the communist government under Chairman Mao, was another period of engagement between Chinese

The YWCA on the Bund, Shanghai, by Lee Gum Poy

architects and their foreign counterparts, but this time, with politically and ideologically aligned Soviet Russian experts.

For a very brief period in the early 1950s, Chinese architects continued their modernist explorations and sought ways for modernist language to engage with China's architecture heritage. However, these endeavours were short lived. From 1952 onwards, the Soviet Union, being the 'Big Brother' of Communist International, became the model for China as far as architecture is concerned. A large number of Soviet architects and urban planners arrived in China as foreign experts to help implement the adoption of Soviet aesthetic ideology, professional organisation, and pedagogical structure.

Soviet architects in China were instrumental in the rejection of modernism and the embrace of Socialist Realism as the principal means of architectural expression. Having already rejected their own modernist and constructivist avant-garde in the 1930s, the position espoused by the Soviet experts was that architecture must be 'nationalist in form, and socialist in content', expressed through the language of Socialist Realism, which in reality took the form of an eclectic historicism, with an almost post-modern use of historic and ethnic architectural motifs, perceived as more humane and engaged with the cultural tastes of the masses. Critical figures such as the planner A.S. Mukhin, the pedagogue E.A. Achepkov, and architect Sergei Andreyev, were the conduit through which the Soviet doctrine was disseminated. The language of architectural expression became a political issue. The fervour the profession had for this newly founded nation and the utopian vision it promised, coupled with a passion for the study and preservation of traditional architecture, led to the wholesale rejection of modernism and the adoption of Socialist Realism. Chinese architects such as Liang Sicheng opened recanted their own modernist tendencies from the preceding decades, and propagated what became the 'Big Roof' style, the pastiche application of traditional Chinese roof forms and decorative elements on modern buildings that were once typically deployed in classical palatial architecture. There were occasional modernist challenges to this orthodoxy, such as the Tongji University dining hall by Huang Jiahua in 1961 and the Qiaobashan Hotel and

The Cultural Palace of Nationalities, Beijing, by Zhang Bo, finished in 1959.

Residences by Gong Deshun in 1960, but these deviations were exceptions in the systemic adoption of the Soviet ideology.

The entire architectural profession was incrementally nationalised and collectivised into a system of state owned and party controlled practices, or Local Design Institutes (LDIs), under which all architects were employed. In a planned economy local LDIs dealt with local commissions most of the time, which meant that competition between LDIs were infrequent, and innovation were not incentivised. When this is viewed in light of the politicisation of stylistic issues under Soviet indoctrination, one begins to see how creativity, which by its very nature constitute a challenge to orthodoxy, can become a dangerous undertaking, with the risk of deviating from party political ideology. Instead, the LDI system were perfectly structured to propagate the standardisation of design solutions with the aim to achieve technical efficiency and conformity.

Simultaneously, a nationwide government led re-structuring of universities based on Soviet models created an architectural pedagogy that resembled a more conservative Beaux Arts-like teaching approach, with an emphasis on technical skills within a prescribed ideology and visual style. The teaching of architecture, which once required the gathering of broad knowledges across the fields of philosophy, science, technology, arts and humanities, was now viewed in a more technical light, almost akin to engineering. A compound result of the Soviet professional practice system and education model is the creation of LDIs that are associated with education institutions, which facilitated the direct transfer of the practically skilled workforce from the classroom straight into the drafting room.

In a remarkably similar fashion to the preceding Nationalist era, the presence of Soviet architects in China was also brought to an abrupt end, following the collapse of the Sino-Soviet relationship in 1960, later followed by the chaos of the Cultural Revolution. Soviet experts withdrew from China and the Soviet doctrine, at least as far as stylistic inclinations were concerned, was labelled revisionist and dogmatic. 'Big Roof' architecture was criticised for its pastiche formalism and frivolity. This provided breathing space for some instances of home-grown rapprochement with modernism, such as Ludiyan Hotel in Guilin by Shang Dun, Sri Lankan National Congress Building by Dai Nianci, and the People's Palace in Guinea by Chen Deng Ao. Nevertheless, despite these instances of deviations in formal experimentation, Soviet models of practice and pedagogy had become entrenched in China, and would go on to exercise influence on the Chinese architecture discourse for decades to come, well beyond the chaos of the Cultural Revolution.

'Starchitecture' and native voices

The end of the Cultural Revolution and the death of Chairman Mao saw China emerge from isolation under Deng Xiaoping's 'Reform and Opening Up Policy' in 1978, and ready to re-engage with the West. After decades of disconnect, Chinese architects now actively sought re-engagement with the western architectural discourse. Pragmatically, there was also a distinctive need for western expertise in the construction industry as China sought to grow its built environment.

It is under these circumstances that western architects returned to China. I.M.Pei was one of the first foreign architects to undertake work in China. His Fragrant Hill Hotel, completed in 1982, offered a nuanced postmodern response to traditional Chinese architectural themes, particularly southern Chinese architectural and garden design heritages. At around the same time, the Jinlin Hotel was completed in 1983 by Hong Kong based Palmer and Turner, and the Great Wall Hotel was completed by American architecture firm Beckett International Corporation, which was the first building in China to utilise a curtain wall system. John Portman's landmark mixed use Shanghai Centre was completed in 1990, one of the first mixed used high-rise retail development in China.

As China's economic activities and pace of development intensified in the 2000s, the design and delivery of increasingly complex and novel new buildings in the commercial, retail, and mixed use sectors required an expertise that frequently could only be fulfilled by foreign architects. Simultaneously, China sought saw the building of major infrastructural, cultural, and civic landmarks as a mean to project its power, prestige and global confidence on the international stage. Events such as the 2008 Beijing Olympics and the 2010 Shanghai Expo catalysed the creation of many iconic buildings of national significance, designed by foreign architects selected for their international renown, technical expertise, and their perceived novel approaches. These ranged from Rem Koolhaas's CCTV headquarters, to Foster & Partner's Terminal 3 at Beijing International Airport, Paul Andreu's National Centre for Perming Arts, and Herzog & de Meuron's 'Bird's Nest' National Olympic Stadium. This was the beginning of what many have since coined the era of 'Starchitecture'.

Similar to previous cycles, foreign influence on the discourse of Chinese architecture in the Reform era went beyond what was built by the foreign architects themselves.

In an echo of the 1920s, the rapprochement between China and the West has facilitated the (re)emergence of a new generation of Chinese architects who have studied and worked abroad, before gaining global recognition for their work in China. Often, the foreign education of these Chinese architects also accelerated the adoption of the Anglo-American studio system in architecture schools as they become involved in the teaching of architectural design. For example, the prominent Chinese architect Chang Yung Ho left China in 1981 on a self-funded scholarship to study architecture in UC Berkeley, and then spending 15 years practicing architecture in the U.S., before setting up the now widely known Atelier FCJZ in China in 1993, later becoming a professor of architecture at Tongji University.

The work of this new generation of Chinese architects are very much a part of a dialogue with their foreign counterparts in China, in which they are asked to consider how their own practice should respond to issues of urbanity, cultural heritage and identity in a rapidly developing built environment. On the one hand, there are those who are heavily influenced by the theoretical and formal approaches of prominent foreign architects. For example, the work of MAD is clearly situated in within the context of the parametricism propagated by Zaha Hadid, under whom Ma Yansong, MAD's principle, had studied and worked. On the other hand there are also those whose positions and approaches have develop precisely to challenge the works of foreign architects. The likes of Wang Shu have developed a distinctively Critical Regionalist approach, rooted in a material and spatial practice that speaks to a sense of place and engages with the construction heritage and the wider Chinese culture. Between these two contrasting approaches, there are a plethora of foreign educated Chinese architects who seek the best of both worlds, deploying the criticality that has informed their western education, in developing innovative solutions to very Chinese problems, without subscribing and succumbing to stylistic straitjackets. For example, the works of practices such as Urbanus are informed by the western discourse in dealing with complex and large scale urban matters whilst adopting a much more nuanced and informed position towards both on identity and place-ness.

The presence of foreign architects in China also forced state owned Local Design Institutes to undertake their own market driven reforms, in order to tackle their own bureaucracy, shortage of technical expertise, and a lack of innovation. By learning from their foreign peers, a process expedited by an accreditation system which forces foreign practices to partner up with LDIs in the delivery

Zaha Hadid's Galaxy Soho looming over the Hutong streets to the south

Red Brick Galleries by Ai Wewei, Cao Chang Di, Beijing

of project on site, the LDIs have transformed themselves and re-emerged as dominant players in the process of both designing and delivering the built environment, able to compete in expertise and innovation with their foreign counterparts and their more nimble and creative domestic peers.

Breaking the Cycle

The preceding sections have shown that despite appearing in seemingly different educational, professional, theoretical and historical contexts, foreign architects have maintained a persistent presence and influence in China for the last century. It is also clear that foreign architects' engagement with China, while persistent, is not contiguous. Instead, there is a recognisable cyclic pattern to the interaction between foreign and Chinese architects. Each 'cycle' begins with the arrival of foreign architects, often with official endorsement, at a critical and transformational historic juncture. They would then go on to play a catalytic role in transferring new technical expertise, introducing new structures of professional practice, propagating new models of pedagogy, and facilitating debates on styles and identity. This is often then followed by the waning of foreign architects' influence and the weakening of their value, ultimately leading to their declined presence.

During the Nationalist era, the arrival of colonial foreign architects was instrumental in the inception of the modern Chinese architectural profession itself. However, as the political tides turned, colonial architects' association with imperialism and capitalism made their position and influence untenable as the Communist rose to power in China after the calamities of the Second World War.

During the Mao era, Soviet Russian architects and urban planners arrived in China and were responsible for the transference of new technical expertise, the introduction of a new mode of practice organised around the LDIs, the adoption of a Soviet Beaux Arts system of architectural education, and the dissemination of Socialist Realism in the formal expression of architecture. However, as Sino-Soviet relationship deteriorated and the chaos of the Cultural Revolution was unleashed, Soviet doctrines were abandoned and the Russian experts withdrew.

The presence and practice of foreign architects in the Reform era have until recent years, fitted into a similar pattern to the preceding paradigms. Arriving in the 1980s, foreign architects have again played a critical role in transferring new knowledge and expertise, establishing new forms of practice, disseminating new pedagogical approaches, instigating debates on style and expression.

Long Museum by Atelier Deshaus, Shanghai

So far, in the Reform era, the relationship between foreign and Chinese architects have enjoyed almost four decades of relatively uninterrupted stability, without suffering any fundamental disruptions or sudden collapse.

Through this prolonged period of engagement between China and the West, a series of issues have emerged which present an existential challenge to the presence of foreign architects in China, who in previous cycles had been perceived as dominant in relation to their Chinese counterparts.

The perception of foreign architects has been distorted in China by the pursuit of 'Starchitecture' in recent years. There exists a quality gap between the design intentions of the foreign architect and the constructed reality, a result of the incompatibility between western construction technologies and a local labour force whose skills at times lie in a very different material culture. The design responsibilities of foreign architects have been fragmented and curtailed by a regulatory system that benefits the dominance of LDIs, both in the structure of the profession and the training of professionals.

At this juncture, foreign architects' expertise, method of practice, stylistic inclinations, and relationship with the state are all being brought into question.

Nevertheless, it would be wrong to claim that foreign architects are now without a raison d'être in China. The emergence of new developmental priorities have opened up new avenues of opportunities for foreign architects in areas where they still retain a great deal of expertise, such as urban regeneration and sustainability. However, these new areas of growth are by no means an indication of business as usual. It is clear that in the coming years, architectural discourse and practice will be driven by the rising voices of a new generation of often western educated, and internationally minded Chinese architects who are leading the search for innovative solution to the challenges of the built environment.

The extent to which this represents to a significant break from past patterns is still debatable, particularly in light of recent geopolitical developments. Over the last two to three years, an increasingly adversarial and rapidly deteriorating relationship between China and the West has emerged. We stand at the cusp where history could either repeat itself or be forced to find a new way forward.

So what does the future hold for foreign architects in China? To answer this question, one must first overcome the common perception that the nature of engagement between foreign and Chinese architects in the contemporary setting is historically unique. As this essay demonstrated, despite distinctively different political, economic, cultural, and social conditions, there is a cyclical pattern of historic interaction between foreign and Chinese architects, in which each period of engagement begins with foreign architects playing an instigative and catalytic role in the evolution of the architectural profession and the discourse, before their influence diminishes as it becomes incompatible with shifting political, economic, and cultural conditions. Foreign architects must recognise that their current role in China is not static, but part of a historical relationship which waxes as well as wanes. Zhu Jianfei's 'Moment of Symmetry' [03] identified a point in time, which Zhu puts around the late 2000s, when the influential position of foreign architects as a legacy of post-colonial relationship begins to diminish, and the flow of influence from West to East begins to reverse, pointing to a shift in the balance of power between foreign and Chinese architects.

As such, a meaningful and relevant future for foreign architects in China will have to be built on the basis of this new power dynamics - a collaborative professional relationship of equals that is able to resist the wider narrative of global balkanisation.

Notes

(01) Marie-Luise Gothein, *History of Garden Art Volume 2*, (Cambridge: Cambridge University Press, 2014), p275
(02) David Jacques, "On the Supposed Chineseness of the English Landscape Garden", *Garden History*, Vol. 18, No. 2 (Autumn, 1990), pp. 180-191
(03) Jianfei Zhu, *Architecture of Modern China - A Historical Critique* (Oxford: Rutledge, 2009), p.170-171

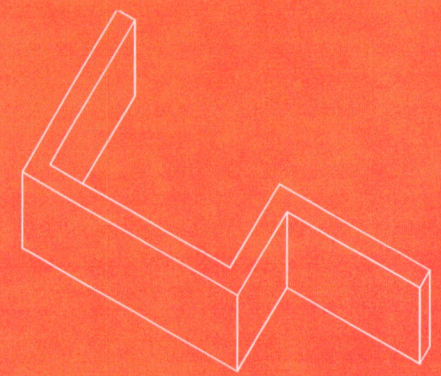

LINEAR BLOCKS

JOHN ZHANG

The linear block emerged in Europe during the *fin de sicle*, and became a prominent and dominant modernist housing type.

Early examples such as the Overstrand Mansions in Battersea, built in the late 1890s, were essentially higher density, taller variations of the terrace typology. However, by the late 1920s, linear blocks such as Edwin Lutyens' Page Street flats were already radically different to their predecessors, almost proto-modernist, where entrances were no longer on the street, but located in a series of in-between, semi-private/semi communal open spaces perpendicular to the street, with flats at higher level accessed from a single core of vertical circulation.

This was the beginning of the modernist idea of the linear block: a high density, high rise edifice that stood over an open landscape, oriented to the light, efficiently planned, infinitely repeatable, with nature and fresh air abound. This was very much Le Corbusier's vision behind Unité d'habitation, as well as Plan Voisin which contained an ensemble of linear blocks, tower blocks and perimeter blocks. Exemplars in London include Erno Goldfinger's Trellick Tower, and Bertold Lubetkin's Spa Green Estate. The Smithsons also explored their ideas of 'streets-in-the-sky' with the linear block typology in the now demolished Robin Hood Gardens. This 'object in the landscape' approach to housing was widely adopted in the UK after WWII in countless council housing estates up and down the country.

The linear block was also widely adopted in China, particularly since the 1950s under the influence of Soviet Russia. The first workers housing community created under the communist government in 1951, Can Yang Xin Cun in Shanghai, is a matrix of two storey short rectangular linear blocks layout at regular intervals with landscaping in between. During the period of collectivisation in 1950s, radical versions of the high rise, high density linear block were created to accommodate urban proletariat communes, such as the Fusuijing building in Beijing. Created from the levelling of an area of traditional Hutongs, the Fusuijing building was an eight storey meandering linear block in which individual and familial lives were subservient to a shared collective life, with communal toilets, kitchen, baths, dining and recreation rooms. In the following decades prior to market reform, housing design became standardised across the country, to the extent that urban dwellers in China today have grown up and continue to live in enclaves of five to six storey linear housing blocks laid out in 15-20m intervals, each of which contains five or six cores, with each core accessing two to three flats per floor.

Our interest in the linear block as a studio is focused on the nature of the relationship between the block and the ground it sits on. Far from the idyllic and almost abstract modernist vision of fresh air and nature, the open landscape surrounding many postwar modernist housing estates in London are often very ill-defined and under-utilised, which frequently led to neglect and misuse. Similarly, the indeterminate nature of the space between the socialist era linear blocks in Beijing have often resulted in its chaotic re-appropriation in the form of make shift private extensions, cordoned off private allotments, informal car parks and dumping ground for rubbish. As such, the meaning and quality of the landscape and the spaces between buildings become critical to the success of the dwellings themselves.

Consequently, the students of the studio, through their work in the following section, have been investigating how the designs of linear blocks and its external communal/public ground can enhance the quality of each other and give meaning to the totality of the whole environment? In most cases, there has been a concerted effort to create a programmatic and narrative relationship between the building and its landscape, orchestrated through novel tectonic augmentations of the traditional linear block. Of particular note are the works of Karol Wozniak and Matt Lindsay, who both sought a new relationship between building and nature, albeit from radically different tectonic approaches.

UP MARKET

MATT LINDSAY

LOCATION: SAN YUAN LI, BEIJING, CHINA

This proposal for live/work studios above a food market is a radical inversion of the conventional relationship between the terrace and the street.

Utilising the linearity of an existing market in San Yuan Li, the project turns the internal street within the market hall itself into the 'street' from which housing above are accessed. Intermittently located stairs at the ground level take visitors onto an elevated walkway overlooking the market stalls. This becomes a second 'street', around which live/work units for market vendors and artists are wrapped. These units, taking the form of an upturned 'L' shape, contain a work/retail space at the same level as the elevated walk way, open to the public. From here a staircase takes the inhabitants up to a dual aspect living and sleeping quarter straddling the full width of the market's footprint, with bedroom on one end and living room on the other. The layout of these studios are inspired by Dogma's model for minimal living, with services and servicing space stacked together to allow for maximum flexibility to the rest of the plan.

From an urban perspective, the seemingly disparate programme of living, working and market are brought together through a carefully considered facade, which is rigorously rhythmic, regular and legible at the ground level, becoming more perforate and playful towards the top, allowing light to drop down through the building.

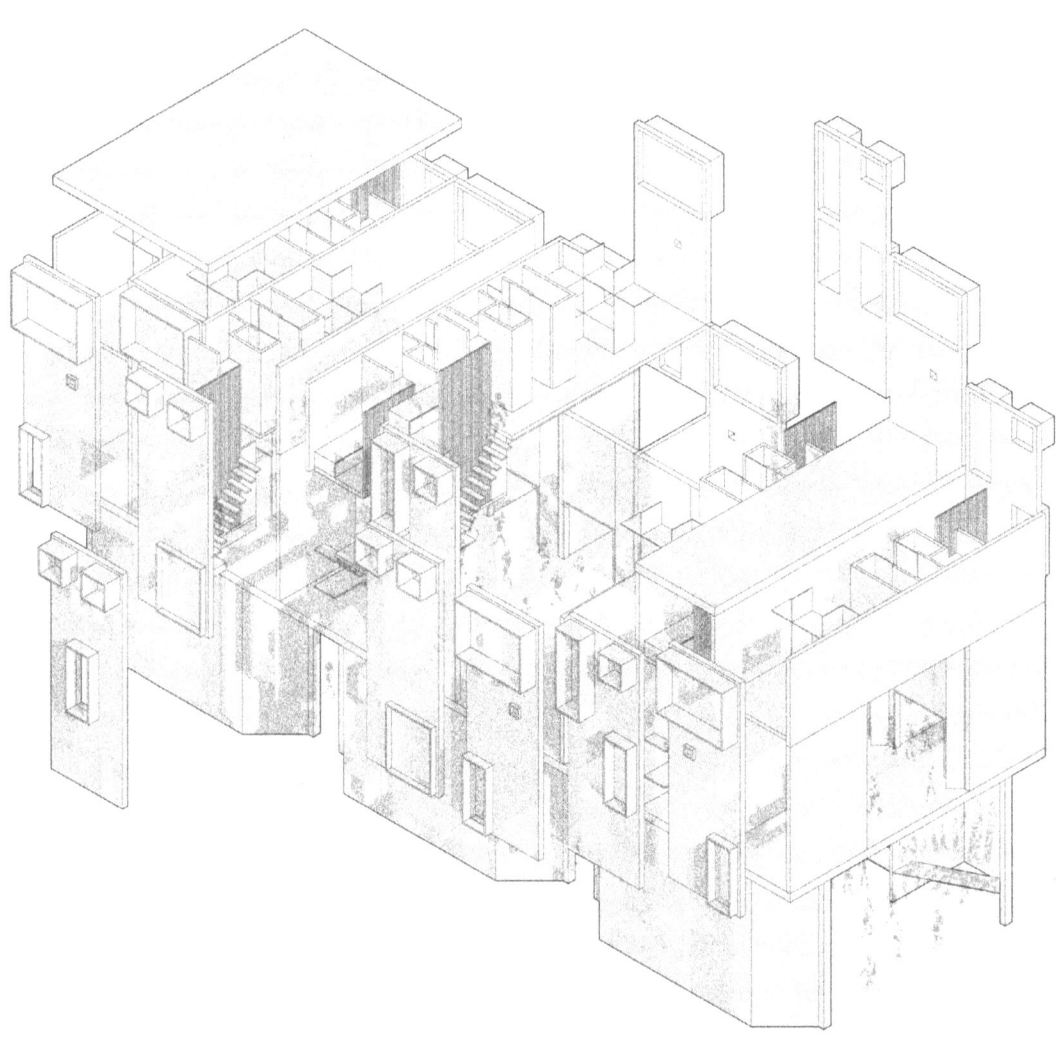

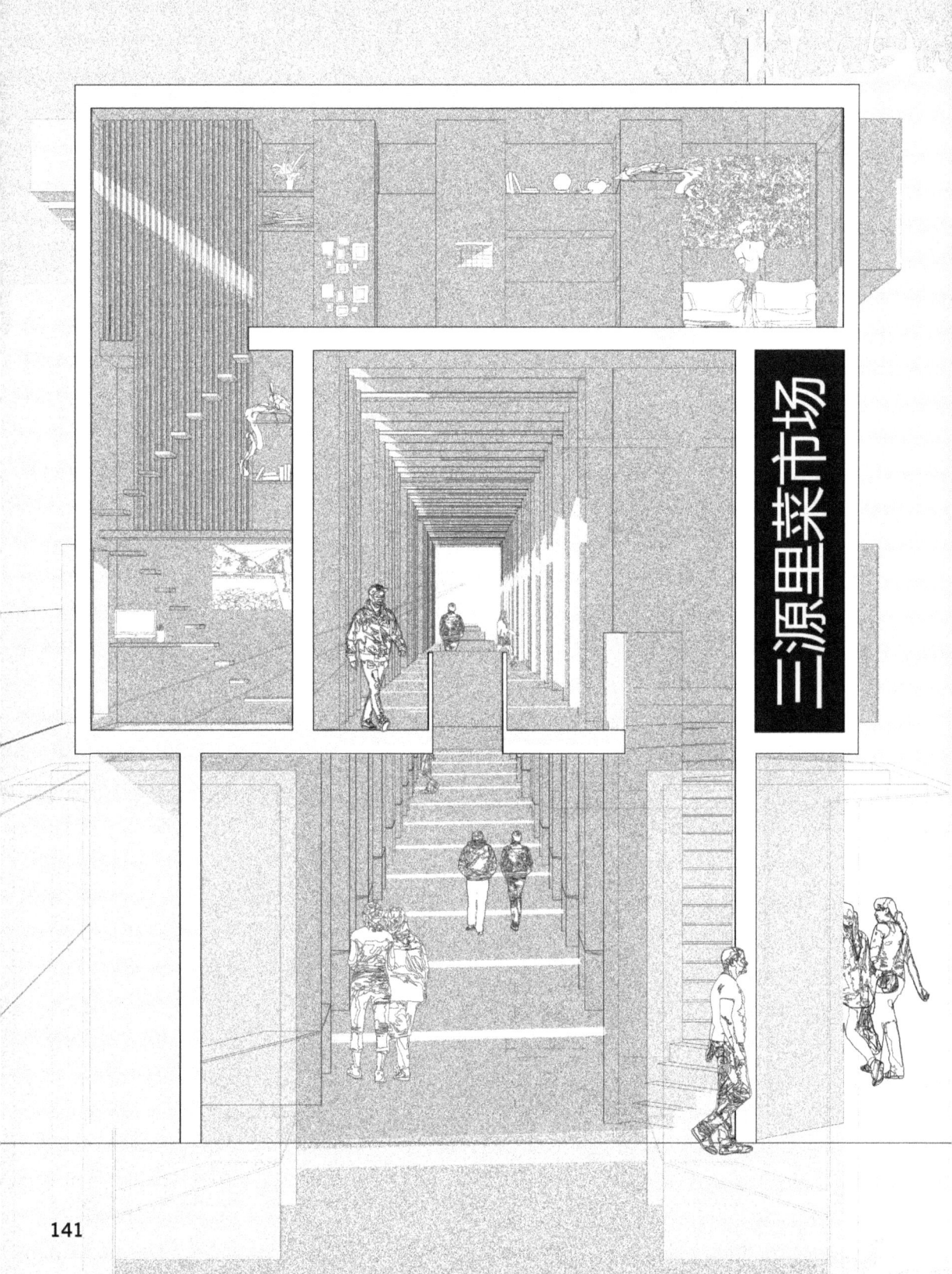

ART OF LIVING

REBECCA COOPER

LOCATION: ROYAL DOCKS, LONDON, UK

This simple proposal of live/work artists studios explore the potential for linear blocks to engage with nature and landscape meaningfully.

On the edge of the Royal Docks, the proposed building sits precariously over the water, with exhibition spaces opening onto the view of the docks. Gentle steps descends from these exhibition spaces into the water, in a gesture to inviting nature into the interior of the building. The landscape quality of the ground level is echoed in the building's vertical circulation, as shallow ramps slowly rise through the rear of the building, leading inhabitants to their respective floors, spaces around the staircase is enlarged at each landing to become a mock-up show space, which, on the first floor, becomes a jetty that reaches far over the water.

Drawing inspirations from Bauhaus precedents, the studio themselves are comprised of a series of double height north facing working spaces that overlook the dock with mezzanine living and sleeping quarters towards the south. The studio spaces are flexibly arranged and offer the artists the option of closing off part of the their space or connect to a neighbour's space. As one move up the building, there are small and subtle variations to this dwelling type. At various moments the studio spaces are taken up by reading rooms, dining halls, or simply a balcony winter garden that look back to nature.

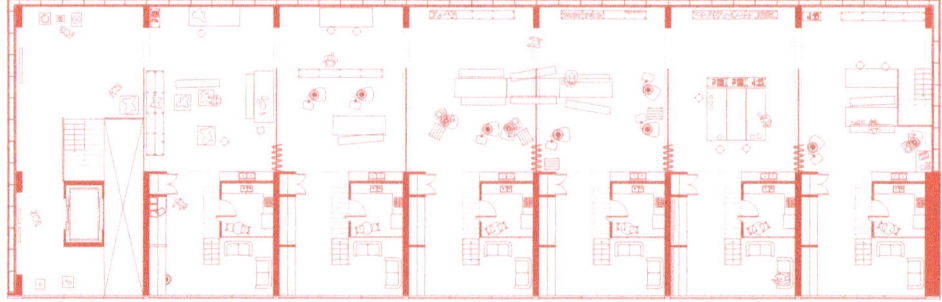

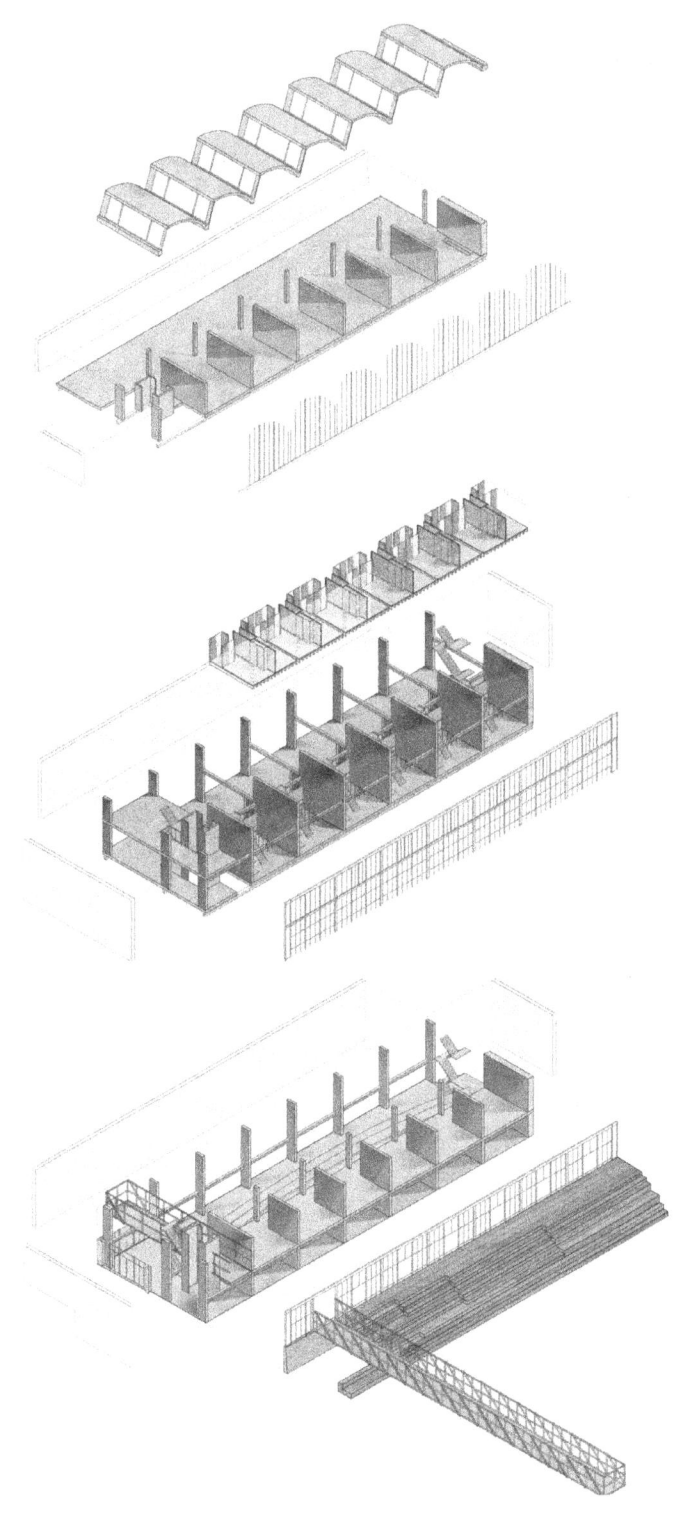

FRAMING BEIJING

PENGFEI GAO

LOCATION: LIAN HUA CHI, BEIJING, CHINA

The relentless efficiency and visual austerity of the linear block becomes the architectural language of subversion in this project that seeks to put the under privileged back into the centre of Beijing.

Addressing the housing crisis facing the urban 'ant-class', a demographic epithet for the highly educated but income poor young people who flock to Beijing looking for their future, the project take inspirations from Dogma Studio's theoretical research into models of minimal living and shared life, and proposes a dwelling type that minimises private spaces and maximised communal programmes. A linear block layout is developed which consists of tightly packed configurations of dwelling units working to a rigorous grid. These linear blocks are then laid out across the site with a variety of generous voids in between. These voids are where the public life of the proposal take place. Large platform-like volumes bridge between the blocks and accommodates a rich range of shared programmes, from dining halls, reading rooms, to outdoor sky gardens. These are the forums in which the inhabitants meet each other, make friends, and form a community. The view from these platform to the rest of central Beijing are framed and flanked by the living units, providing the inhabitants with a sense of place. This ensemble of slabs and gaps are sat on a plinth, below which the public is allowed to move through at will, encouraging the engagement between this vertical neighbourhood and the rest of the city.

OLD AND YOUNG

HUGO SHACKLETON

LOCATION: LONDON BRIDGE, LONDON, UK

This projects explores how the linear block can be de-constructed to allow different forms of communal life to penetrate its spatial order.

The project consists of three linear housing blocks for multi-generational families sitting on a raised plinth overlooking a park in south London. The communal life begins at the scale of the dwelling, where, inspired by informal Chinese precedents, two independent apartments for a young family and the grandparents share a common entrance area and a double height cooking/dining/playing area. From these apartments, the residents can move up to the covered roof terrace, where there are reading rooms, rooftop allotment gardens, and gyms. The plinth on which the linear housing blocks sit becomes a shared entrance garden for all residents, whereas below the plinth, within the semi-buried under-croft contains a crèche, sports pitches, and rooms that the young families can hire for birthday parties and meetings.

From both the under-croft and the plinth, gentle steps and ramps slowly takes residents and visitors into the park. Thus the urban narrative of the project becomes clear, one of a continuous journey from the park to the super attic, along which the private realm, the communal realm, and the public realm interweaves seamlessly.

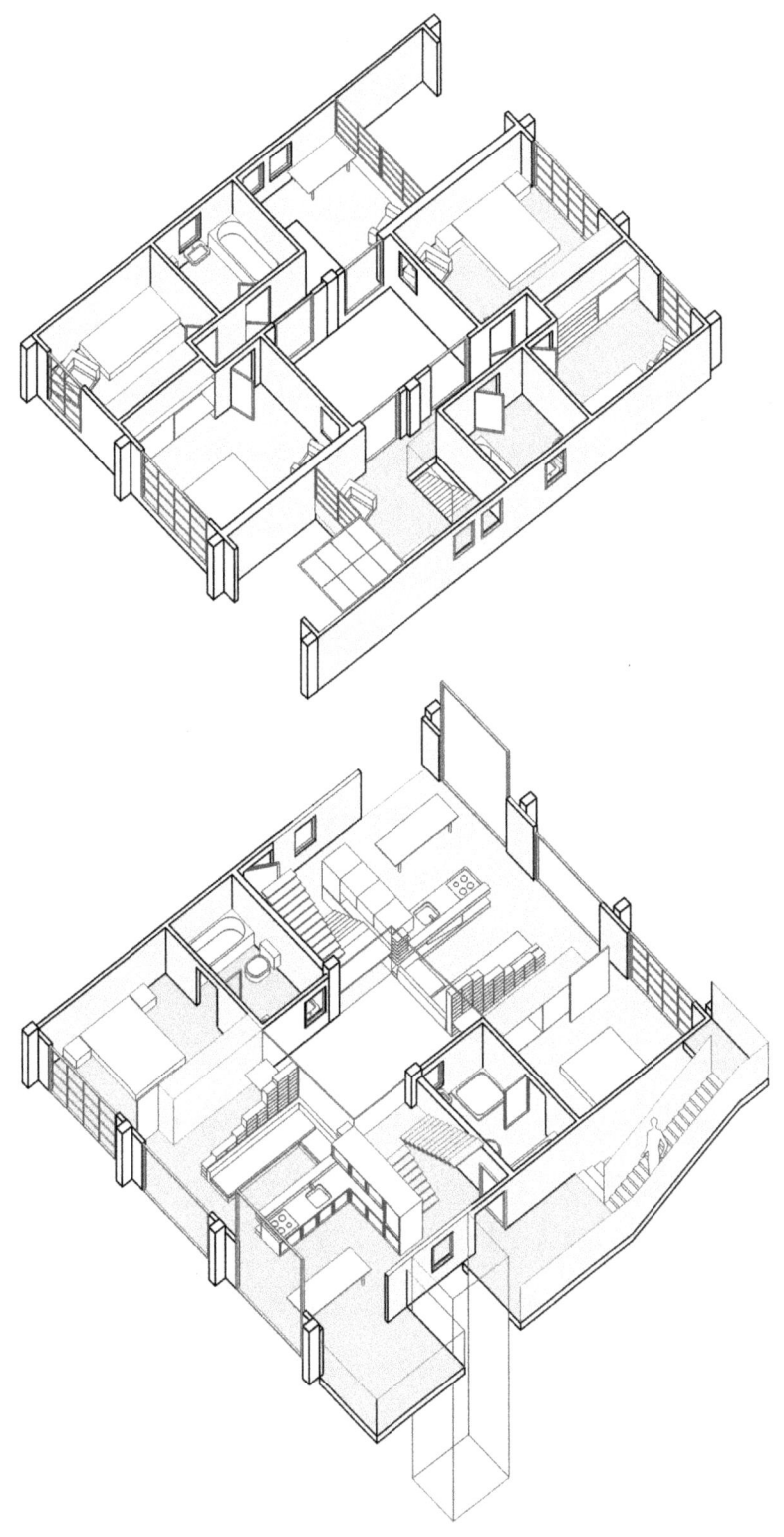

VERTICAL CO-HOUSING

ARIS JONES

LOCATION: HOLBORN, LONDON, UK

This is a deceptively simple re-interpretation of the terrace housing type, but in its simplicity is a richness of adaptable flexibility and porosity that allows it to accommodate a variety of lives.

Developed to occupy the empty street edge of a council estate in Holborn, the proposal is based on the repetition of a simple modular plan working to an alternating grid of narrow and wide spaces. In the centre of the plan is the core, around which two 'L' shaped duplex family apartments are wrapped, each dual aspect and offering double height spaces. This basic order of space and apartment types are then manipulated at various parts of the building to create bespoke moments of shared delight.

At the top of the building the duplex apartments become single storey barrel vaulted flats with a shared roof terrace, which sits over the top of the lift core. At the mid-level of the building, the duplex family apartments become duplex couples apartments and the freed up double height space becomes a communal dining hall that can be used by residents to host parties and gatherings. At street level, accommodation is omitted, save the room immediately adjacent to the core, which becomes communal storage spaces. The rest of the ground floor is carved out to create a tall and generous underpass, giving access to the communal garden beyond. The overall urban effect is a rhythmically composed and permeable urban frontage that re-establishes the identity of the street.

LIVES OF ARTISTS

BRYAN ESPINOZA

LOCATION: LONDON BRIDGE, LONDON, UK

This housing project for artists in London Bridge examines the linear block housing type in context of the Open Building principles of pre-fabrication and adaptability.

Inspired by Metabolist precedents and ZAO's modular plug-ins in Beijing's Hutongs, the project imagines a construction system of a permanent concrete grid framework, into which pre-fabricated modular duplexes, built from cross laminated structural timber panels, are inserted. Each duplex contains double height live/work space and an external balcony. As these units begin to fill up the concrete superstructure, some 'slots' are left empty. These void spaces becomes full of future potentials. In the immediate and near future, these spaces becomes spill over studio spaces for the artists that form this community, where they can move from the interior of their individual duplexes onto these double height external voids, and use the space for the preparation of larger pieces of artwork, or simply to grow vegetables, play ping pong, or dry their clothes. As the community grows, some of these 'slots' could easily be in-filled with more pre-fabricated dwelling units. This idea of flexibility and adaptability is also reflected in the building's urban gesture at the ground level, where a concrete under-croft is created to allow the public to freely pass through under the building, meandering between flexible gallery spaces made in timber that can grow and shrink as the curatorial calendar of the artists change.

  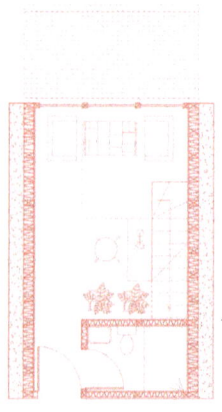 

VERTICAL KINKS

SHI ZEYUAN

LOCATION: LONDON BRIDGE, LONDON, UK

This project re-imagines the linear housing block as an interplay between private dwellings and a continuous landscape of communal activities.

With its back against the street and facing onto a public park in London Bridge, the proposal consists of a cranked linear block that sits on a raised plinth which gently emerges out of the landscape of the park itself. Criss-crossing ramps and shallow steps take visitors from the greenery of the park onto the raised public podium, which contains a generous south facing cafe terrace overlooking the park. From here one could either descend down into an under-croft art gallery facing the street or move up through the lobby to the dwellings above.

The dwellings themselves consists of two variation of a dual aspect split level typology, where dining, sleeping, and eating happen on different levels, connected by stairs and views to the park, with balconies overlooking the greenery below. This layout avoids having circulation corridors on every floor and maximises visual amenities.

In an inversion of the arrangement seen in exemplars like Unite d'Habitation, spaces for communal activities, such as libraries, gyms, meeting rooms, have been fragmented and distributed along the circulation route as one move up the building, creating a dynamic journey, a punctuated facade, and communal life that intimately engages with the private dwellings that make up this neighbourhood.

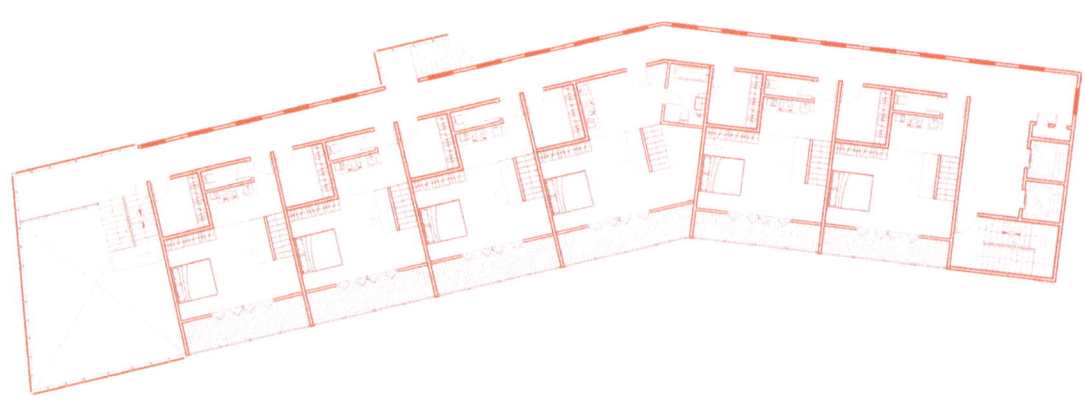

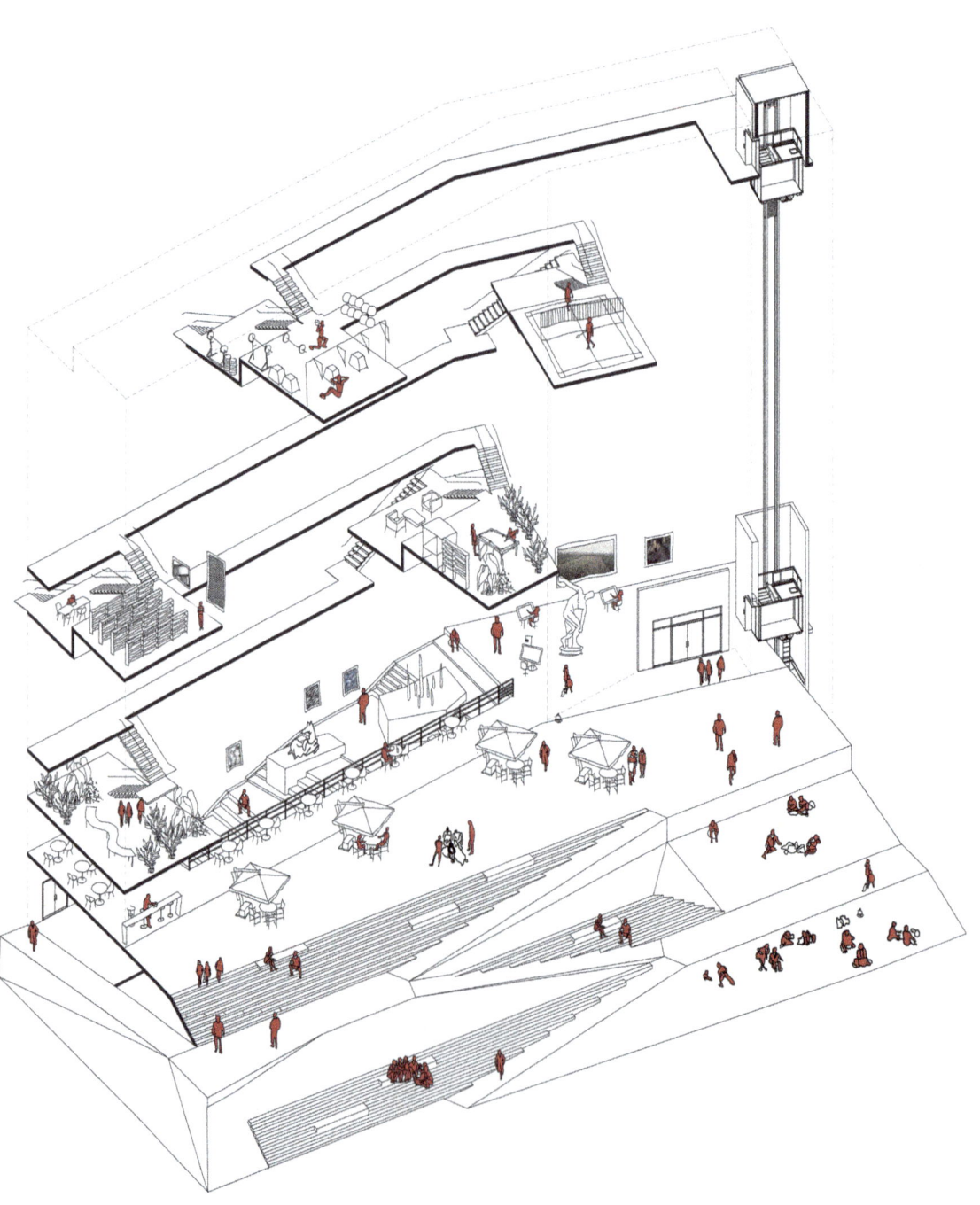

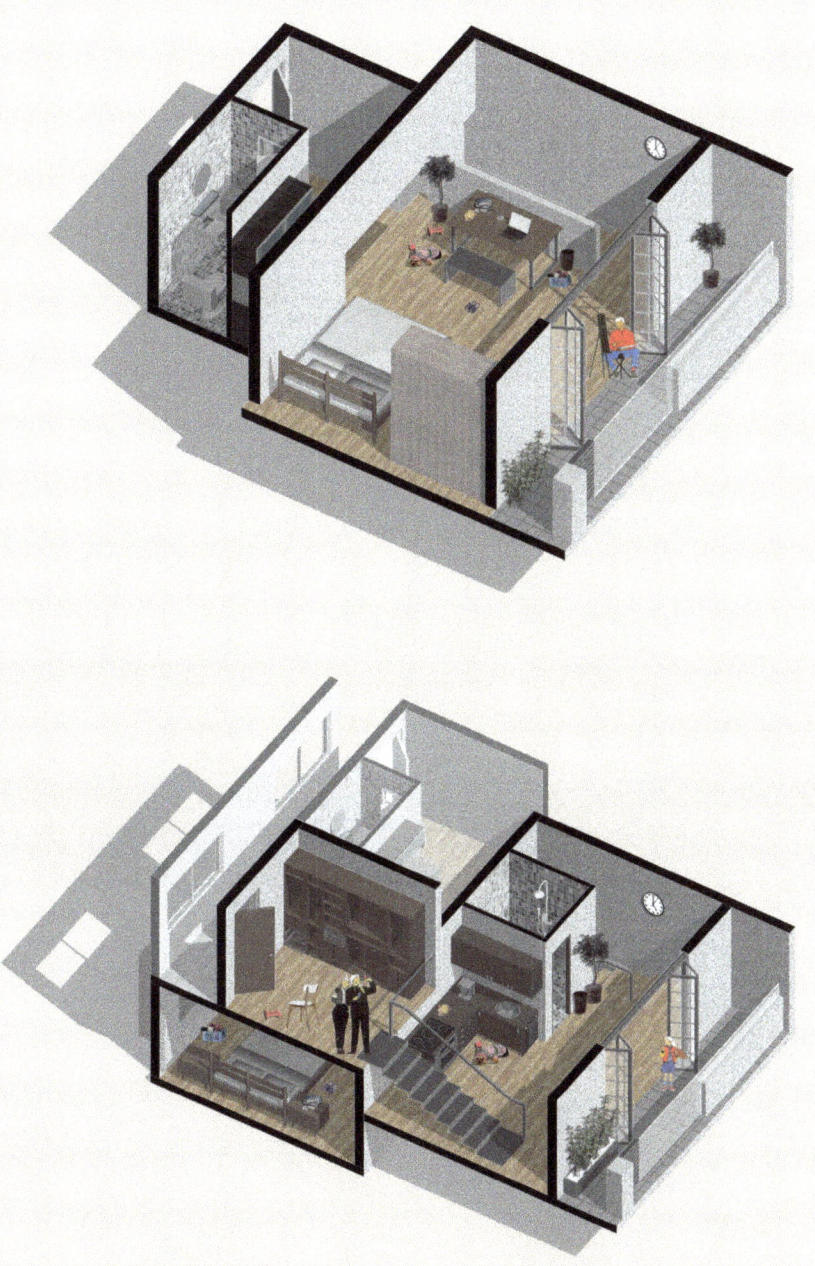

LANDSCAPE THERAPY

IRINA BODROVA

LOCATION: LONDON BRIDGE, LONDON, UK

This is another exploration of the relationship between the linear block and the landscape it sits on. The proposal experiments with the idea that the building and the landscape can be considered to be the same thing.

In developing a topography that seeks to use the landscape as a form of therapy for vulnerable recovering patients, the project takes inspirations from the inversion of the interior and the landscape in Chinese rammed earth dwellings, and to a lesser degree the typology of Chinese courtyard. The result is a meandering linear block that follows the street pattern and almost, but not quite, encloses the perimeter of an 'L' shaped site.

Five storeys high on its prominent north-westerly street corner, the linear block drops in height incrementally as it moves around the perimeter of the site, until at the southeast open corner, the building's roof is at the same level as the external landscape, and the block effectively disappears into the ground.

This tectonic move means that the roofscape of the entire building becomes continuous with the landscape at the centre. Within this topography, simple lateral dwelling units are arranged to overlook a lower ground spa, which consists of a series of indoor treatment rooms surrounding a group of outdoor thermal lidos. From there, a gently rising landscape take residents slowly onto the roofscape, which effectively becomes a linear park that traverse the entire perimeter of the site.

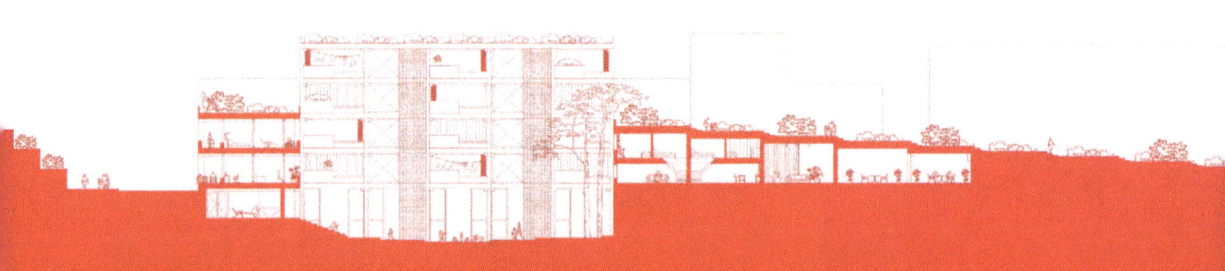

NATURE-HOOD

KAROL WOZNIAK

LOCATION: LONDON BRIDGE, LONDON, UK

This is a highly innovative exploration into the diversity and sustainability that can be integrated into the linear housing block through various techniques of hybridization.

Inspired by the Warner terraces in London, and Hans Kollhoff's Piraeus housing project in Amsterdam, with ideas of an expanded realm of privacy in the Chinese Hutongs, the project is a complex collection of dwellings conceptually brought together through a narrative revolved around the idea of the garden.

3 dwelling types, a duplex apartment, and a terrace house made of a pair of stacked flats, form the fundamental building blocks of the proposal. Each type is designed with its unique outdoor green space, be it a sunken courtyard, back garden, or a double height planted balcony. These units are organised within a snaking superstructure that sit over the site in south London, whose meandering form establishes street frontages, frames public access through the site, and creates a communal garden.

The narrative and presence of nature permeates throughout the scheme. From the private moments of greenery within each dwelling, generous walkways are flanked by facades of living green walls, which leads the residents to the community garden at ground level. Moving up, the living facade folds into a dynamic covered roofscape, where there are allotments and play spaces.

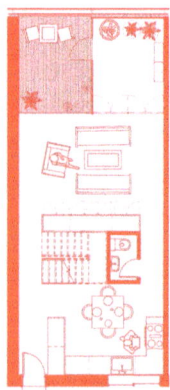 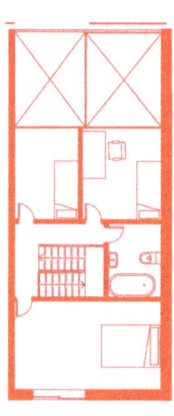 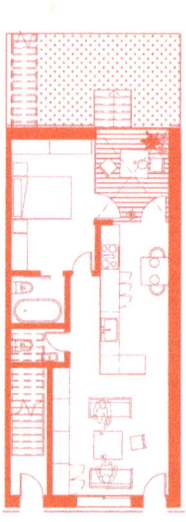 

UP THE WALL

YUFAN XIE

LOCATION: HOLBORN, LONDON, UK

This is a highly innovative conceptual exploration of the linear block as a wall that connects rather than divides.

Conceived as a project that re-stitches a scattered site in London, the proposal creates a singular mega-structure that meanders through the site. At four storeys tall, the 'inhabited wall' is in fact an extremely porous structure with an open ground floor consisting only of supporting shear walls and stairs, leaving the footprint largely free for pedestrians to traverse and cross with ease.

As one ascends the 'wall', a series of apartments, some over a single level, some duplexes, open up along the staircase as projections from the wall, in a play of solids and voids, creating a composition of indoor and outdoor spaces. Within this overall tectonic approach a surprising variety of housing types are created, ranging from studio units for students, to family homes for 5 people. As one reach the top of the continuous staircase, flooded with top lit light, one emerges onto a roof terrace, which is accessible to all of the residents within the inhabited wall. This becomes a linear park that connects all of the units and creates a sense of community.

From an urban perspective, as the mega-structure dances across each part of the site, it begins to introduce an overall coherence to the various Georgian, Victorian, and modernist housing fragments that already exist on site.

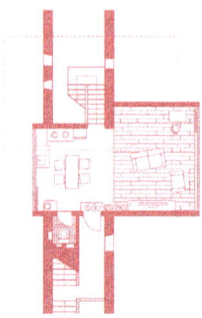 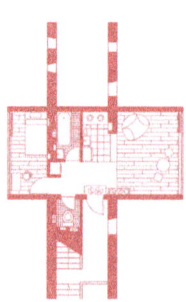 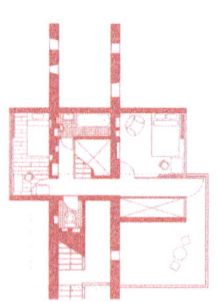 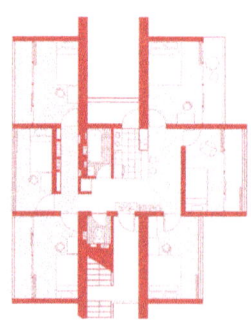

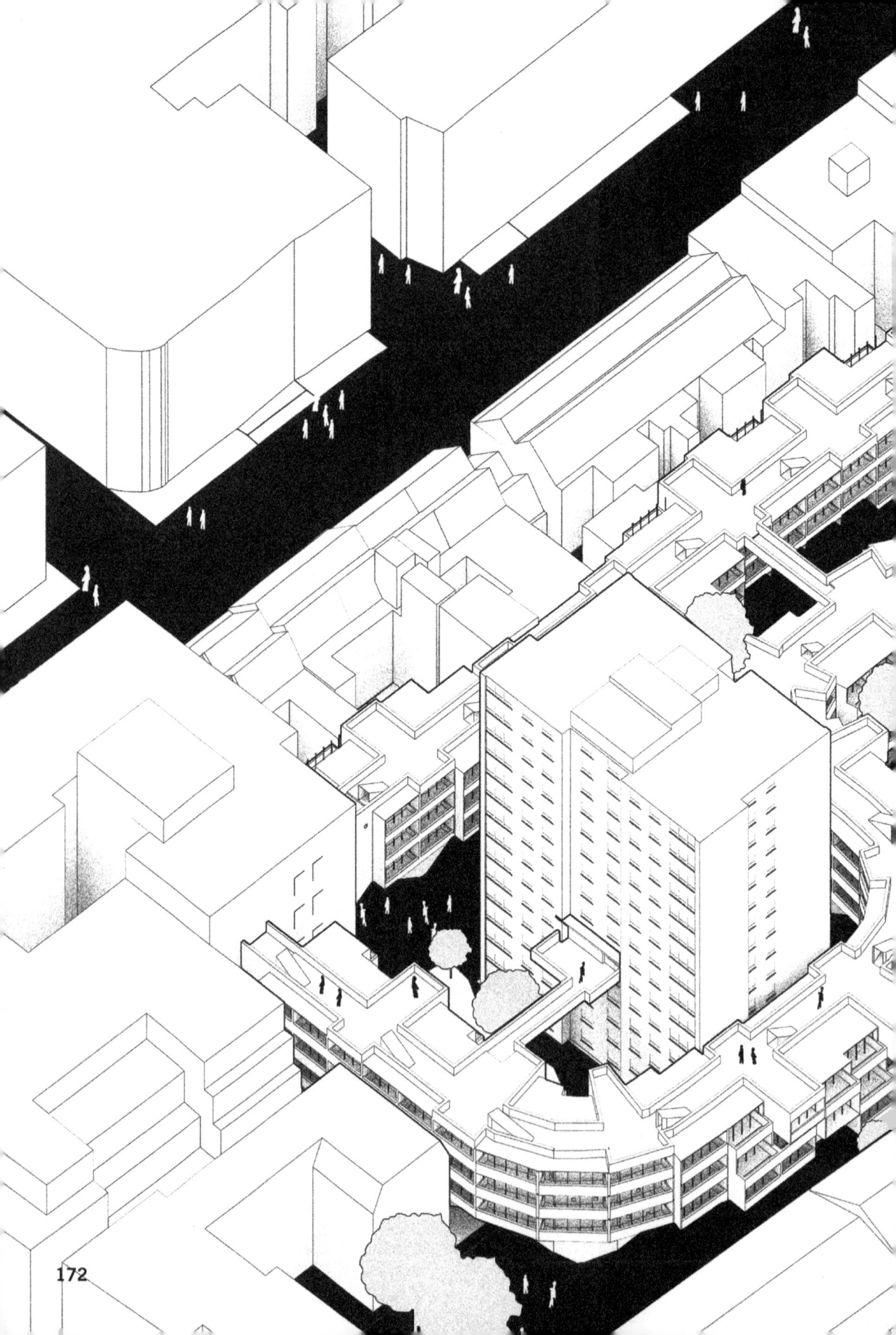

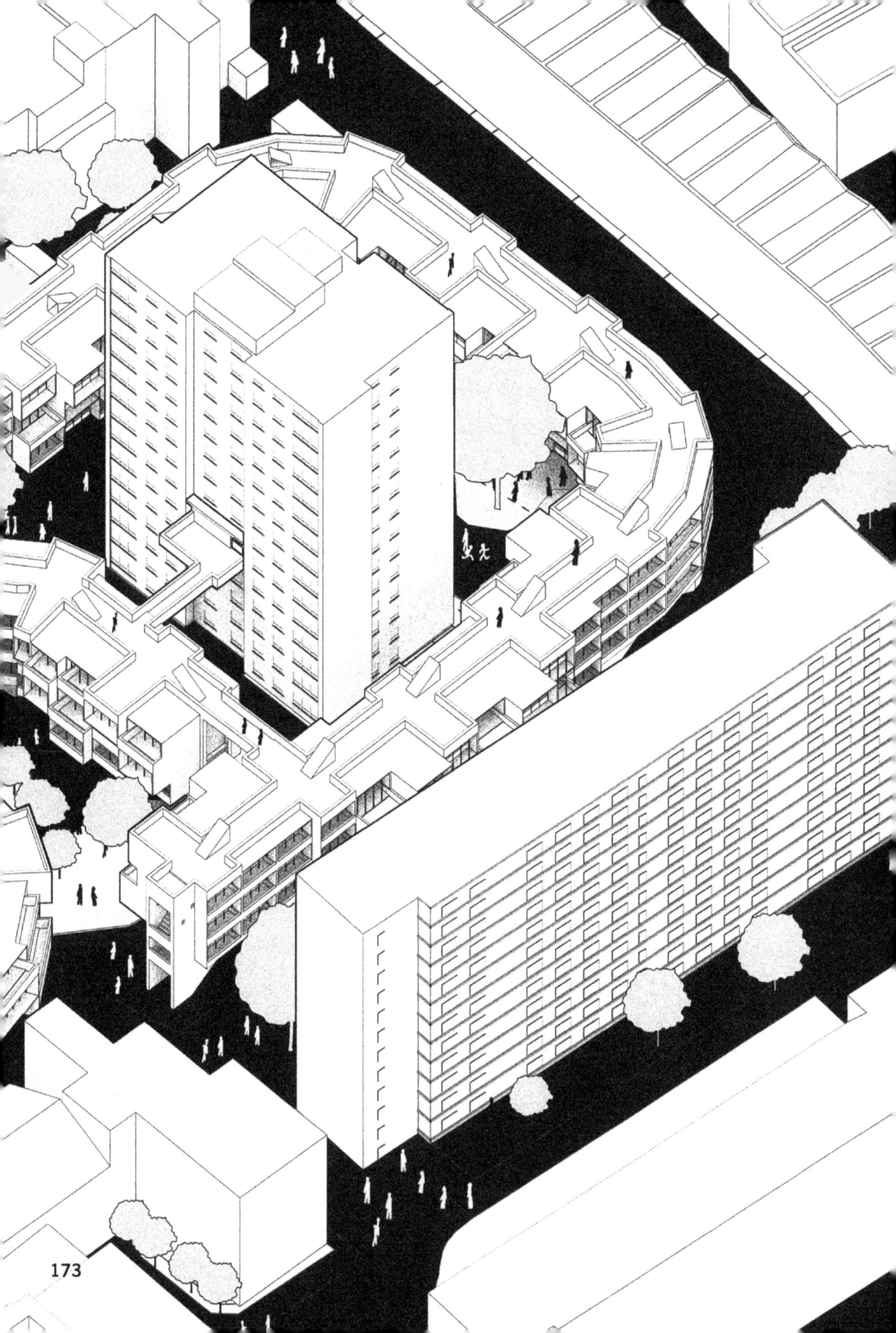

A MONUMENT OF MINIMAL LIVING

MATT LINDSAY

LOCATION: LONDON BRIDGE, LONDON, UK

This project considers the meaning of monumentality intrinsic to the tectonic qualities of the linear block.

Heavily influenced by Aldo Rossi's Galleratese Quarter, the Cambridge Cripps building by Powell and Moya, and P.V. Aureli's speculations on minimal living, the proposal consists of a meandering linear block held off the ground by a tall colonnade.

The linear block is principally occupied by a compact, dual aspect, one bedroom studio dwelling type, developed in response to the increasing number of young, single and transient people arriving into the neighbourhood in Somers Town. To further integrate these new arrivals into the neighbourhood, the colonnade allows the public to move freely under the building, turning the space enclosed by the building into a welcoming neighbourhood park. The landscape plays on the Chinese idea of borrowed views amongst structure and nature. A series of communal programmes aimed at the wider neighbourhood is located at various parts of the building's interior, inviting local residents to visit. This creates a condition where the building becomes a piece of 'infrastructure' for both the residents and their neighbours.

Indeed the project is imagined as a monument that seeks to give the communities in Somers Town a renewed sense of identity. Thus the proposal meanders beyond the boundary of the site, bridging over roads and dissolving into the neighbourhood.

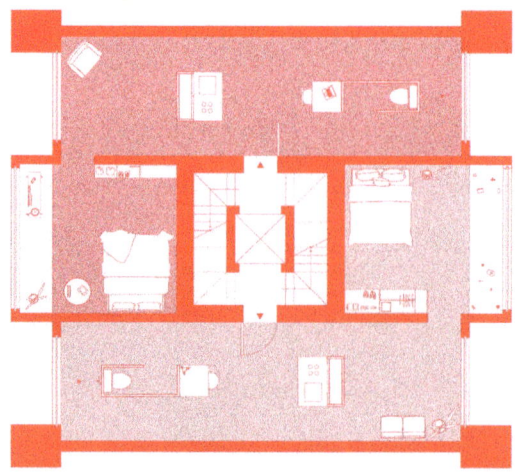

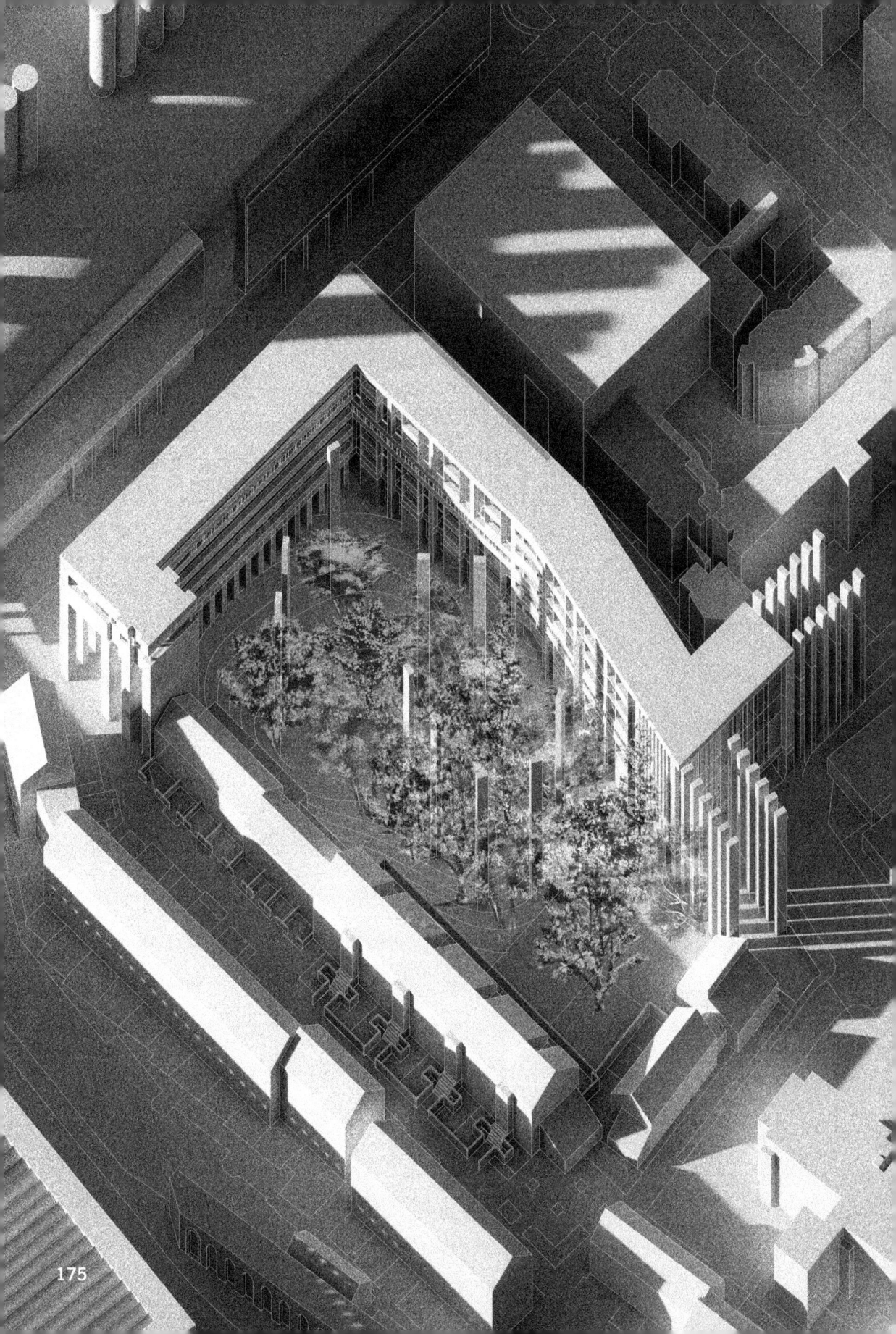

ON A COMPARATIVE PEDAGOGY

JOHN ZHANG, DAVID PORTER & KEREN HE

JZ: The programme of this studio does not easily fit into the nominal model of undergraduate architectural education in either UK or China. I know of no other undergraduate studio in the UK which engages with a global partner at the same depth and length. Speaking from your respective global settings, to what extent does the studio reinforce or challenge the prevalent pedagogical structure in its methods and topics? Keren, is there any equivalency to other studios in China? David, what do you make of the differences in the required learning outcomes between students from China and the UK?

KH: CAFA is always fairly open for collaboration and communication with other schools and institutions worldwide. Before the International Exchange Studio, I had been involved in many joint workshops and exhibitions which were, however, mostly supplemental to the nominal curriculum. I think other universities in China have the same circumstances. The studio's intensive joint program is embedded in our curriculum, which I think is unique and can be considered an experiment for architectural education. Modern architectural education in China started in the 1920s and arrived by way of Europe, the U.S., and Japan. The earliest education systems in schools in China were originally either the Beaux-Arts model or the Polytechnic model. After a century of evolution, architectural education in Chinese schools began converging. Today each school has its own reformed and collaborative approach, but most schools' core curriculum appears to be very similar. The lack of diversity in education has become a key issue. Hopefully, our experiment can trigger some reflections on the pedagogical structure.

DP: One of the big changes in the organisation of Higher Education in Europe has been the introduction of explicit 'Learning Outcomes'. Each school has to carefully describe not just what the students should learn, but the depth of knowledge they are to achieve. Of course, what students learn is not the same as what teachers teach, so this approach assesses not just the effectiveness of a student's learning but the effectiveness of the teaching programme in achieving its stated aims. The government provides a template for the drafting of these Outcomes, but it is up to the school to interpret them creatively.

The question of what topics architecture students have to learn is covered at the European level and is unsurprising. It includes designing buildings, of

Professor He Keren's lecture on public space in Beijing

course, but also architectural history, urbanism, environmental and structural design and so forth. But the kind and depth of the knowledge acquired by the student, their 'cognitive skills' is not subject specific. In principle an undergraduate student of architecture is meant to achieve an equivalent intellectual level as an undergraduate student of mathematics, philosophy, literature or chemistry. The combination of subject-specific topics with cognitive skills provides a more forensic approach to assessing what students have learned and, at the same time, a more forensic approach to assessing whether a teaching programme is achieving its aims. It provides the means for shared discourse between teachers within and between schools, and the means to explore and make improvements to the programme. It also provides the basis for students to evaluate their own progress.

When I was first at CAFA I had discussions with Dean Lü, influenced by his experience of the European dialogue, about introducing this approach into CAFA. But I don't think it has been followed. The case against this approach is that it is bureaucratic, but the positive case is that it focussed discussion to enable if the be more precise than therefore more creative.

JZ: I can think of several novel aspects of our joint studio which make it a rather unique pedagogical model and endeavour.

Firstly, whilst across the world academic and pedagogical exchange in architecture are becoming increasingly common place, it is still rare, certainly amongst UK architecture schools, for exchange programmes to be this extensive and immersive. Over the 8 weeks that the UK students spend in Beijing, they slowly become embedded in the city. This is not a group which develop designs for an exotic location from the comfort of their London studios based a fleeting visit. They become familiar with the site and its people by visiting again and again. The excitement of being in a radically different cultural context seems to bring out the adventurousness in them. Each year, with the help of their Chinese counterparts as translators, the UK students have been able to carry out interviews with local Beijing residents in the enclaves that they are researching, something that rarely happens back home!

Over the years, students have been invited into people's homes to share dumpling meals and look into their heirlooms – the most intimate moments of daily Beijing life.

Secondly, through its comparative agenda, our studio asks students to work on not just one, but two sites, in Beijing and London. For the students of the China studio, the programme does not follow the conventional undergraduate 3rd year path of a smaller architectural intervention which expands into a larger more substantial project. Instead, the year is divided equally by location, into two equally significant housing proposals. The project in Beijing is often actually by density and scale the larger of the two. This 'throwing into the deep end' asks students to quickly overcome their procrastination and engage in 'thinking through making': reflecting on their assumptions, hypothesis, and ideas through physical acts of drawing, collaging, modelling, filming and even building. The intensity of this process often elicit the most intuitive responses in students, which often turns out to be the most insightful and interesting – the plan and section diagram they're asked to draw in the first week in this accelerated mode are often the most lucid and potent versions of their ideas.

From a teaching perspective, the comparative brief and the extended trip to China presents their own challenges in terms of ensuring that the UK students are still able to satisfy their commitments to other teaching modules back in London, such as the technical study, cultural context essay, and preparing for practice modules. As graduating students, there is a rigorous framework of learning outcomes they must satisfy. However, by and large, they have risen to these challenges. It is particularly interesting to see the crossovers between design and writing, where their stay in Beijing have inspired them to pick up topics relating to Chinese architecture in the written dissertation, some of which have been very insightful.

There is also an interesting technological angle to this. For several weeks of the exchange programme, I am away back in the UK whilst the students continue their work in Beijing. In order to ensure their progress is consistent with what is expected of them back in London, a system of weekly remote Skype tutorials has been developed. The preceding week's work is sent to me digitally and shared on screen during the Skype session, this allow us to talk over drawings and do 'live' digital mark-ups spontaneously, as in a face to face tutorial. Skype also allows the tutorial session to be recorded so the conversation, and the marking up of drawings can be played back later for the students to take more extensive notes. This is where digital media, technology, and the internet come together to aid in new ways of remote teaching. In this regard we seem

The students at a public consultation in Fu Guo Li, Beijing

to have pre-empted the post-pandemic mode of virtual learning adopted across the world.

JZ: A key ambition of the studio is to engender creativity through a comparative pedagogical approach. Critical to the success of this goal is the art of selecting the right sites from both Beijing and London, where critical insight can be developed out of similarities as well as differences. Keren, what have been your experiences of this process and the consequent outcome in the students' work?

KH: At the beginning of the programme, the sites we chose for students to work on were quite large, especially when we work on the real project. The scale of the site could be considered typical for a "Chinese scale" project. For instance, in the fall semester of 2015-16, we worked with a design institution to research and renovate an auto shop complex in the southwest of Beijing; a very large site. Even after we scaled down to only one block the site was still relatively large for the students and difficult to comprehend, particularly to the Europeans who were used to working on projects with a much smaller scale. Gradually we learned to reduce the size of the site to a reasonable scale, making it more manageable for both CAFA and European students.

JZ: It was certainly revealing to see the scale of site that students in China typically have to contend with. For me the frequency at which the Chinese students deal with such context has given them a sense of confidence and some competence in responding to issue of scale and density. This is clear to see when the CAFA students are in the UK working on London sites. Whereas their UK counterparts might be rather over-cautious, they are not afraid to imagine scenarios where sites can take on more density and intensity. Conversely, it is also interesting to see the UK students' approach to site in China, where their initial intuitive responses tend to be much smaller in scale and lower in density, often the combined result of their Eurocentric sensibilities and the romanticizing of traditional low-rise Chinese courtyards.

From my perspective, I'm always looking at how the Beijing site and the London site compare to each other. Ideally, we always want some similarities so it encourages the transfer of ideas, but at the same time we also want some element of contrast in order to expose differences which can lead to a widening of knowledge base and design palette. The auto shop complex site in Beijing was vast, the UK students really didn't know how to handle a site of that scale. In contrast, in the same year, the London site was a small car park in Southwark. Beside from a tenuous connection to cars, there really was very little the two sites had to say to each other. We've gotten better over the years however, both in the scale of the sites and the context around them. For 2019, we looked at an existing housing enclave centred around a community green space in Beijing. In London we examined a piece of Somers Town, where post war housing surrounds a community park. The scale of the sites were much more comparable, with similar developmental context, all of which led to a much more meaningful transfer of ideas between first and second semester in terms of the proposals produced by the students.

JZ: In many ways, the exchange students' design intuitions have been honed by their immersive experiences in another country's architectural culture, which opened up new perspectives and inspired new ways of thinking. Have you seen evidence of a meaningful transfers of knowledge through the work of the students? What has been carried over as they move from one location to another? Conversely, what differences has been revealed in the design sensibilities of students from China and the UK as they tackle two radically different contexts?

KH: The most important quality for the people in the studio, including the teachers and students, is to always have an open mind. Each year we have our CAFA students from basically all over China. Our exchange students are mostly from Northern Europe - from Scandinavia, Germany, and Switzerland - and occasionally some from Southern Europe (i.e.: Italy) and some students from other Asian nations, such as Japan and Korea. And the Westminster students from the UK are actually from all over the world as well—Britain, Eastern Europe, South America, etc. It is always interesting to see how all these various cultures meet in one room. From the beginning you might see obvious differences, students from different cultures and schools would show different characteristics in their ways of learning, thinking and design. For instance, students from Scandinavian schools are usually very keen on their concept from the beginning and persist with it throughout; students from German and Swiss schools, who are more technologically oriented, are really careful of how things are put together; Westminster students from the UK are very driven in their step-by-step approach from research to design; and our CAFA Chinese students are normally not overly enthusiastic in expressing themselves but prefer to be quite practical and are exceptional at drawing. However, the joint program is also a process for the students and teachers to learn from each other, not only academically, but culturally too. During the Beijing semester, we often organize a lecture series regarding Chinese architecture, landscape and urbanism for the students to get to know the local culture. Having this kind of mixed team in the studio is one of the biggest advantages of the program.

DP: Thinking about creativity, one of the characteristics of creative people is their ability to see what you and I see, but to see freshly and see deeper into things, and so come up with new thinking. This applies to scientists as well as artists and architects. The Exchange Studio is the ideal vehicle for seeing things afresh, because so much is new. I think the real challenge is to the quality of looking and the questioning that should, for a creative person, accompany looking. Looking, really looking, is very hard work. Watching images on a screen is no preparation for looking at the world. Indeed, it is probably harder for this generation to look at the world, than any generation before them. The art of looking needs to be re-learned as a critical tool. Browsing is not looking. One of the most difficult things to learn is to learn how to see – an appropriate challenge for an architecture department in an art school.

JZ: Speaking more practically, from what I see students produce, there are certainly ample evidence that what they do in Beijing is finding its way into London. Perhaps the most explicit example is how the courtyard typology is being explored in the students' proposals over the years. The Siheyuan courtyards have inspired students not only to seek reinventions of it in their work in Beijing, but also test how the same spatial arrangement of buildings organised around a central outdoor space can be adapted in the climatic, urban, formal and material context of London. In 2018, our student Signe created an extremely complex pattern of interconnected courtyards separated by cloistered linear housing units which intersected each other and shared certain facilities at the corners. Critically, she was able to contextualise this typology into a very London specific narrative of re-stitching the in between spaces in under capacity post war housing estates. The transfer of ideas isn't restricted to forms, types, and materiality, but also ideas of privacy, of social interaction, and of density. Students are particularly fascinated by the much more blurred boundaries between the private and the public realms in Chinese

Students speaking to local residents at the Shijia Hutong Museum, Beijing

cities, which provides them with a valuable point of reference to question the accepted spatial definitions of privacy back in the UK. The sign of success is when an idea from Beijing which is initially crudely tested in London through the simple act of copy and paste, but then developed or 'remixed' in order to adapt to local conditions, until something altogether original emerges.

JZ: As far as teaching methods are concerned, the studio also deploys several novel techniques which requires thinking through making. In Beijing, the residential project is often preceded by an exercise in which students produces a model/sculpture/artefact by reading and interpreting a critical text. In London, the students are often asked to make a piece of film as a way to analyse and understand a site/space/community. What do you think are the goals of these exercises?

DP: We are talking about the idea of "thinking through making" here, which is one that is very strong in the British art and design tradition. To put forward a very simple view of architectural education, there are two main Western traditions. One being the Beaux Arts tradition, imported into the USA from France, and by chance picked up in the Chinese education system. From my perspective the Beaux arts is more academic and concerned with issues of composition, style and theory, but less engaged with building and with society. On the other hand, is the arts and crafts tradition, which includes the Bauhaus, where the underlying principle is learning through making, where the touch and feel of things is important, where 'thinking through making' is critical.

KH: We start each semester by carrying out a short exercise. We ask the students to read certain narrative texts related to cities and architecture, and then represent the texts in various forms of visual media, such as drawings, sketches, photography, collages, models, video, installations, etc. The cross-cultural reading list includes Italo Calvino's Invisible Cities, Murakami Haruki's Hard-Boiled Wonderland and the End of the World, the Chinese classic Story of the Stone, and the new award-winning science fiction novel Folding Beijing. We believe it is an interesting and valuable exercise for the students to try to think as artists, learn to connect literary work with visual interpretation, and explore more techniques in architectural presentation.

JZ: For us, film making has become an important tool to introduce the studio to the idea of thinking through making. The depiction of the built environment in films has long been a topic of academic exploration. As architects we are fascinated by them as they make explicit the temporal and narrative nature of our relationship to architecture and the city. In Falling Down Michael Douglas' recently unemployed white collar worker takes a walk through different neighbourhoods of LA as his mental state deteriorates, in which the city is revealed to us almost as a 'section' cut by the steps of the protagonist. In Jia Zhangke's The World, the surrealism of replicate versions of architectural icons from around the world forms the backdrop to the tragic stories of migrant workers trying to make it in Beijing.

However, what is far more interesting for me is the ability of films to reveal something about the relationship between people and the space around them. William H Whyte's The Social Life of Small Urban Spaces is an excellent example of how by simply observing with camera, one becomes aware of certain patterns of use and interaction between human beings and their environments. Indeed this is what we asks the students to attempt every year through their films, a simple piece of observation that reveals certain insights about the site.

I'm also interested in how films make us pay closer attention to the intimate spaces around us. In Wong Karwai's In the Mood for Love, we feel that we know the dimly lit alleys covered in old and torn posters as well as we know the human characters. In Yasujiro Ozu's films, the camera's eye level drops to that of a person sitting on the tatami, from where the viewer is clearly aware of a Japanese spatial culture. So we ask the students to also try and uncover stories about a place and a community through their films.

JZ: Engagement with the real world of buildings and the reality of practice also feature prominently as part of the studio's pedagogical approach. In London, I recall the students seeing Neave Brown in his Fleet Road home, visiting the studios of Sterling Prize nominated Feilden Fowles, and being critiqued by writer and architect Douglas Murphy. In Beijing, there were field trips to the offices of Zhang Ke's ZAO and Ma Yansong's MAD, with critiques from OPEN Architecture's Li Hu and Wang Hui from Urbanus. What value do you put on this kind of engagement and what are your criteria for choosing who to engage with?

KH: Visiting offices is always the most popular part of the programme during the Beijing semester. On the one

Model making workshop for UK and CAFA students

hand, the aforementioned architectural practices are all quite successful and well-known to most of our students, who are always quite keen to see how they work in reality, on the other hand, these outstanding architects are also quite connected to CAFA. Most of them like Wang Hui and Li Hu are frequent guest critics of our studio. This semester, Li Hu and Huang Wenjing from OPEN Architecture will have their own experimental studio in CAFA, where we will begin to share facilities and critiques with each other. It is always important to keep the balance of practice and teaching.

DP: Meeting architects and visiting their offices has been important. Seeing architects engaged in similar questions to the ones we were asking in the studio, and being paid by a client to do so, comes as a revelation. Architecture becomes something tangible, not an abstract game. Real people design real buildings that get built and this changes a small bit if the world. Visiting Neave Brown in the housing project that he built back in the 1970's was a real highlight. Neave Brown is not a star architect but is being rediscovered by a younger generation of architects quite simply because of the quality of his work as built and inhabited. This is not through stylish websites but through completed buildings that can be visited with residents who anyone visiting can talk to. They are not 'virtual'.

JZ: We think it is incredibly important that, for a studio exploring housing, the students should engaged with the reality of practice. Over the last few years, the London sites have all been real plots slated for housing redevelopment. In 2018, we looked at the Tybalt Estate redevelopment site funded by Camden Council. In 2019, we worked with a site in Somers Town in the middle of phased regeneration, where we brought in the architects in charge of the masterplan to explain to the students their design principles. This year (2020), we have been be working closely with Lewisham Homes on a site in the middle of redevelopment near New Cross, where we engaged with the commissioners of social housing on the processes of feasibility studies and master planning. This is accompanied by invited professional practitioners and academics who are engaged in housing design and issues concerning housing. Edward Simpson, a senior architect from Karakusevic Carson, well know for their innovative housing projects, was a regular critic of the studio. Douglas Murphy, writer and architect, who has an expertise on post-war modernist architecture in London, including experimental housing projects from the time, is another regular critic to the studio. Through these provisions, the students have been able to engage with real world scenarios, and indeed this is precisely why candidates are attracted to our studio every year in the application process.

JZ: The goal of teaching is ultimately to facilitate learning, but in David's words, learning is really 'just a higher and more purposeful level of thinking'. Here, then, is where different ways of thinking affect how we learn differently. China and the West inherits radically different traditions of thinking, and the act of thinking itself can also manifest through both theory and practice. Has the exchange programme revealed any insight to you in terms of your understanding of the philosophy of learning?

KH: When I look back over the past five years and I think about the programme I realise we have learned much more than we anticipated. Not only did we learn how to do urban and housing design, we also learned to think differently. It is vitally important to have an open mind in today's world. For instance, over many years of teaching we have observed that Chinese students tend to think quite similarly and aren't always keen to express differing opinions. The reasons are complicated, which we believe are mostly due to culture and education. We ourselves were educated in this same way. Through the intensive collaboration and communication in our studio, everyone has the opportunity and circumstance to step out of his or her comfort zone, explore beyond his or her custom way of thinking, break cultural boundaries and get inspired. Ultimately, finding his or her special talent and capacity and thereby gaining more confidence, rather than losing it. We've had a strong start and are hoping to keep it that way.

JZ: I think I would come back to David's earlier idea of learning as thinking and thinking through making.

As someone who received his architectural education in the early 'naughties', I am acutely aware of how the very acts of looking, thinking, and therefore learning has changed radically. There's been a major shift in the way we interact with the object of our gaze and contemplation: the process of looking and thinking are now mediated by the internet, smart devices, social media, and new digital technologies. We take photos of buildings with our smartphones, put it through stylising filters digitally via different software, and post them onto our social media feeds, to be then consumed by others. Architecture is now consumed as images via

Instagram, so much so that clients now asks architects to make sure that their buildings are 'Instagramable'. The consequence is that we are constantly looking and thinking through the lens and agencies of others, be it our devices, our Facebook friends or some AI algorithm. We have become so used to it, that students start to equate research with 'googling' for perfect images of architectural 'precedents', from lists curated by algorithms that second guess your preferences.

This is what we must confront in the way we teach in the future, how to engage our critical skills as designers to look and think through acts of drawing, collaging, photographing, modelling, film making, and other new and exciting means made available by technology. This is perhaps why the exchange programme and the comparative methodology is interesting as a teaching model. It is precisely in the visceral encounter with the unfamiliar, as when UK students arrive in Beijing, and vice versa, that they become aware of their own human agencies to access their subject matter directly, and their ability to produce insights by simply confronting the physical reality of the new and looking at things afresh.

DP: We started without an agreed and explicit method or objective. Only through working together can we get to the point of reflection, where looking back, we can see what we (teachers and students) have achieved together, working through trust and interaction.

The cultural and generational differences between the three of us have enriched the studio. John was born in mainland China, then transposed to England, has studied architecture in a world dominated by Rem Koolhaas and Zaha Hadid, is digitally literate and just finished his PhD. Keren is a Beijinger who studied and then worked in the United States during the post-modern period of the 'new urbanism' the returned to be one of the first generation of architecture teachers at CAFA and is undertaking a PhD supervised from Paris. I am a Londoner who became an architect because I went to a school designed by Walter Gropius, have taught all over the place, built a lot, and when I started studying architecture Le Corbusier was (just) still alive. Never did the PhD.

We have communicated using the English Language, and so have our students, but with a range of different accents. This has made us all the more careful about how we explain things. Although designing is predominantly about the use of visual media to develop

Studio visit to Feilden Fowles offices

Students practising Xu Bing's calligraphy at the UCCA exhibition in 798, Beijing

and explain ideas, we use words too. It is evident to me that the medium for representation inevitably influences and limits what can be represented. It determines for us what we can imagine.

A long time ago I asked Ron Herron, one of the founders of the Archigram group and fantastically skilful at drawing by hand, whether there was anything he could imagine but not draw – he replied no. Imagination and representation are bound together. The means we use for representing our thoughts are not neutral in the role they play in creativity but influence what and how we think.

Thinking about my Chinese students in the studio, the forward-looking dynamism of China means there is a sense that almost anything is possible. This is wonderfully invigorating. Things seem to be reinventing themselves, including the possibilities for architecture and architects. This is wonderful, but there is also a difficulty faced by the Chinese students – if almost anything is possible, and architecture seems to have few limits, then what exactly will they do? Is there some central core to the art of architecture, or do we do what we like? Where are the limits and what are the core skills?

Parallel with this ready embrace of the new, there is a nostalgia for a lost past. 'Tradition' has been a word that I heard often in Beijing. Perhaps a sense that something is being lost, something essentially Chinese? One of our Chinese students in the exchange studio latter came to study in London. At CAFA he had been part of a small painting group who would take easels into the countryside and paint at the weekend. His paintings had a freshness and life about them. I spent a lot of time talking to him at CAFA about how you look at things when you are painting them, and how different that is from looking at a painting. In London I asked him if he was still painting and he said he had given up his brushes and was painting digitally now. He showed me his work which was technically sophisticated but, for me lacked freshness and depth. Something was gained but something was lost. It would have been interesting for me if he had pursued both means of painting, exploring the old medium against the new one. Not replacing one with the other.

I spent 11 years teaching at the Glasgow School of Art and there was a continuing concern there about the responsibility of artists, architects and designers, encouraged by teachers but often lead by students. There was always a strong social responsibility but increasingly an environmental one – what is our responsibility to society, our planet and the future? Looking back, this kind of thinking was always present in the exchange studio, but I would hope as it progresses these ethical questions of responsibility become more central.

A MOMENT IN BEIJING

SIGNE PELNE

A STUDENT'S PERSPECTIVE

For me, travelling and exploring matters. So when the offer came to live and study in China as part of the Joint International Design (JID) Studio, I jumped at the opportunity. And so my final year at the University of Westminster started with a heavy suitcase and a plane ticket to China.

I remember my first day in Beijing. Tired, sleepless and famished from the long journey, we set out on our first sojourn. The urban characteristics of the area around the CAFA campus looked strangely familiar for someone like me who had been brought up in post-communist Latvia. Still, this was the furthest away from home I had ever been, Beijing was going to be my new home for the next couple of months. I had promised myself to last through the day without sleeping, so caffeine and walking were essential. After finding our first meal we set foot in the Hutongs and began to explore. The Hutongs, which serve as the streets between the traditional Siheyuan courtyard houses, immediately impressed me with their vibrancy. Saturated and messy, they are a perfect example of the spatial intimacy generated from communities with strong bonds amongst its residents. The alleys were often taken over by street vendors, bicycles, Chinese chess games and impromptu circles of elderlies trading gossip. People and connections mattered here. Beyond the traditional grey brick walls, it is glimpses of the internal courtyards you yearn for. Occasionally, I got a chance to venture inside the courtyards and come close to these intimate personal landscapes tucked away behind the walls, each one made unique by the families sharing the space.

In the weeks that followed, I continued to explore, walking along the congested roads of Beijing. We talked our way past the security guards at Steven Holl's Linked Hybrid, tried our best to get past the tall fence around the secretive CCTV Headquarters by OMA.

Beyond these widely known iconic buildings, we uncovered other gems like Riken Yamamoto's Jianwai SOHO, a group of buildings oriented against Beijing north-south urban grain, sitting at an angle to allow greater public permeability. These mixed-use towers had sunken gardens: a 'below the ground' strategy which also became the inspiration behind my design explorations. Beijing was more than just 'Stararchitecture'. We also visited the poetically muted architectural projects of Ai Weiwei in the Caochangdi district, wandering in awe at the simplicity of the tactile materiality of his buildings, each one restricted to a limited palette and laid with sensitivity to the

The international studio cohort from 2018

landscape and the construction culture of the area. Soon after, deadlines settled over our heads like the occasional Beijing smog, and we spent our days frantically turning our impressions and interpretations of Beijing into architectural experiments. I confined myself to the CAFA campus, dashing between my dorm room, the studio, canteen and bar. As someone who had not dealt with housing design up to that point in my education, I had to learn from first principles how to design homes that responded to a complex context in a sensitive manner, all the while being aware of the culture I was designing for. This was the beginning of a realisation that housing design was deceptively challenging, it would require a great deal of empathy and insight from us all to understand how to design for a community that we were not yet familiar with.

Through conversations, tutorials, visits to local Beijingers' homes, our ideas began to crystallise. Taking inspiration from the existing Hutongs, I aspired to make a project, which at its core would address the issues of loneliness and community in contemporary Beijing, to bring human connection back to the block housing communities, similar to what I had noticed among the existing Hutong communities.

When ideas dwindled we went back out into the city looking for inspiration. There was an entire country to explore beyond the gates of CAFA. Trips to the Summer Palace reminded me of the gentle and tactile approach of traditional Chinese architecture, which impressed with its sensitive and thoughtful use of landscaping, constantly playing between the simplicity of scarceness and abundant wonder. Thoughts also turned to grander urban realisations, such as finally noticing the strange 'flatness' of Beijing, where there are no buildings of significant height in its centre, which further accentuating the importance of the Forbidden City and Tiananmen Square, a condition evolved out of a rich history of political, cultural and even military agencies. There was also the trip to Shanghai, whose international and cosmopolitan identity stood in contrast to Beijing, where we indulged ourselves in colonial era monuments, contemporary galleries and art spaces.

After a mind-boggling two months of architecture, friendship and fried dumplings, we said our goodbyes to Beijing and its people. Like with any place I visit, the goodbyes were marked with a melancholic feeling of some unfulfilled goals, of more places I wanted to see in China, sowing the seeds for another trip in the future, I hope.

Back in the UK, it was natural for us to apply the lessons we had learnt in Beijing, to what we were designing in London. My final thesis work, a tapestry of infill courtyards for a 1960s council estate, was heavily influenced by the Chinese courtyards. My project drew on the intimacy and conviviality of the Siheyuan, as well as its sparse and minimal materiality. Critically, informed by my architectural experience in China, I began to seriously question our received wisdom on the threshold between the private and the public. Chinese architecture made clear to me that between the very public street and the privacy of our living rooms, lies the possibility for an endless trail of in-between spaces. These take the shape of informal outdoor furnitures, doorsteps, corners, courtyards, covered walkways, colonnades and even the makeshift vegetable gardens clinging onto electricity poles in the Hutongs. These were places for lingering and socialising. I began to see how important it is for architecture to leave room for the undefined and nuanced interactions between families, neighbours and strangers - architecture as a mean to create human connections.

In the time between my exchange and writing these reflections, I have finished my bachelor studies, completed work experience and have already started my master at the Royal College of Art. Each one of these experiences has allowed me to engage within different ways of thinking about architecture, and the endless complexities of the architectural discourse. Yet the Beijing experience still resonates with me. I think that within architectural education it is very important to expose yourself to as many different outlooks and ideas as possible. As confusing and contradictory these discourses may seem, it has helped me to develop an awareness for divergent perspectives. The JID Studio has made me leave a lot of preconceived notions of cultural 'norms' behind, and develop a much more informed view on the world. So, travelling and talking to strangers matter. Two months was not enough to untangle the curiosities of Beijing. I can only keep on travelling, reading and hoping that more students keep on wondering and learning from the different and the seemingly strange.

Signe Pelne *is a former student of the JID Studio 2018-19. Her project in Beijing and London were nominated for the AJ Student Prize. She worked for Hawkins Brown after graduation and is now finishing her MA in Architecture at the Royal College of Art.*

The students at ZAO Standard Architecture's Micro courtyard project in Dashilar, Beijing

PERIMETER BLOCKS

JOHN ZHANG

The perimeter block has long been a fundamental component of settlement design, the origins of which is sometimes attributed to fortifications with a more defensive outside and a softer and more secure private inside for its community of inhabitants. The outward public fronts and the inward private back constitute the essence of the perimeter block, which is clearly discernible in the historic quadrants of the Oxford and Cambridge colleges.

Given this definition, one might even argue that the London terrace, which tectonically is more akin to the linear block, when placed back to back and bounded by four streets, forms its own perimeter block. Of course more explicit precedents exist. The Eixample district of Barcelona, designed by Cerda definitively illustrates the principles of the perimeter block. Closer to home is London's Dolphin Square, which at the time of its construction, according to Nikolaus Pevsner, was the "largest self-contained block of flats in Europe". It inverts the traditional Georgian garden square model by moving the private communal garden within the perimeter of the block and pushing the streets beyond its boundary.

The modernist movement in housing largely eschewed the perimeter block typology, in favour of the linear block or the tower block model, both of which championed the object-in-a-landscape approach to housing. Le Corbusier did include perimeter blocks in his seminal Ville Radieuse master-plan, but only on the periphery of the scheme. The Plan Voisin had no perimeter blocks, even though the part of Paris it sought to replace had plenty. This was the case in the UK, even at the Barbican, where there is a wide range of tectonic variations, the wrapped linear blocks along the edge of the site never quite connect or continue to form any full enclosure. Cadbury-Brown's World's End Estate in west London was one of a few exceptions, but even here the corners of the perimeter have been hybridised with tower blocks. In recent decades however, there has been a renewed interest in the exploration of perimeter block in housing, exemplified by the masterplan for the 2012 London Olympics Athletes Village, and individual precedents such as Peter Barber's Grahame Park project in north London.

As a studio with a global perspective, it is important to acknowledge that despite the above history, the perimeter block is neither an exclusive western or urban concept. The Fujian Tulou for example, is a multi-storey doughnut shaped free standing building that accommodates entire clans of hundreds of people in rural south eastern China, the oldest of which dates as far back as the 14th Century. For the Tulou, its perimeter form differentiate the ground into an enclosed courtyard for ancestral worship and communal activity, and a landscape beyond is working agricultural land.

Despite their radically different evolutions and settings, what is common to both the Tulou and its European counterparts, is their ability to, through their intrinsic tectonic qualities, clearly define a set of private, public, and communal spaces, which can then be meaningfully programmed. In this sense, the perimeter block is no longer necessarily a continuous volume, but an urban ensemble of forms which must, through their internal tectonic logic, collectively decide how they want to cohere to or differentiate from the city. Such endeavours often require critical rethinking of both the tower block and the perimeter block typologies. Steven Holl's Linked Hybrid in Beijing presents an innovative experiment in this regard, where a community of residents in a group of tower blocks are physically linked through a series of programmed bridges at high level, whilst the ground is given over to the city with cafes, a cinema, and a park.

The work from students in this section are very much preoccupied with the perimeter block and its creative augmentation. They have been particularly interested in how new communal spaces beyond the main enclosed ground floor space can be created. Of note are the works of Remi and Rebecca, whose proposals are hybrids of tower blocks and perimeter blocks, with fascinating uses of the extruded voids within to create moments of sharing.

24 HOUR BLOCK

ANISSA COLACO DE SOUZA

LOCATION: LONDON BRIDGE, LONDON, UK

This project explores how the enclosed and inward looking nature of a conventional perimeter housing block can be overturned via hybridisation to actively address the city around it.

Conceived as housing for hospital key workers who often come off shifts late at night and are on call 24/7, the proposal brings in a variety of non-residential programmes and spaces into a tectonically simple four sided perimeter block containing 2 dwelling types, resulting in a rich strata of different activities throughout the building. The perimeter at the ground floor is lined with a re-interpretation of the terrace house for key worker families, with their front to the street and their back giving access onto private gardens and a communal allotment garden. The roof of these terrace houses form a continuous raised podium which can be accessed from the street via a gentle set of wide steps. Sheltered under a colonnade, above which are more duplex apartments for single occupants, the podium engages with the city through a series of round-the-clock programmes: 24 hour laundrettes, all night diners, late night barbers and convenience stores. This is where residents and their colleagues from the hospital, as well as locals employed in the night time economy come after their shift for a bite to eat, a glass of wine, or simply a chat whilst they wait for their clothes to dry.

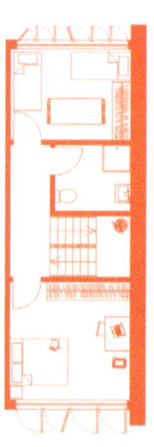
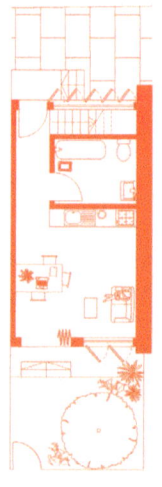
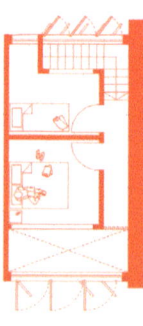

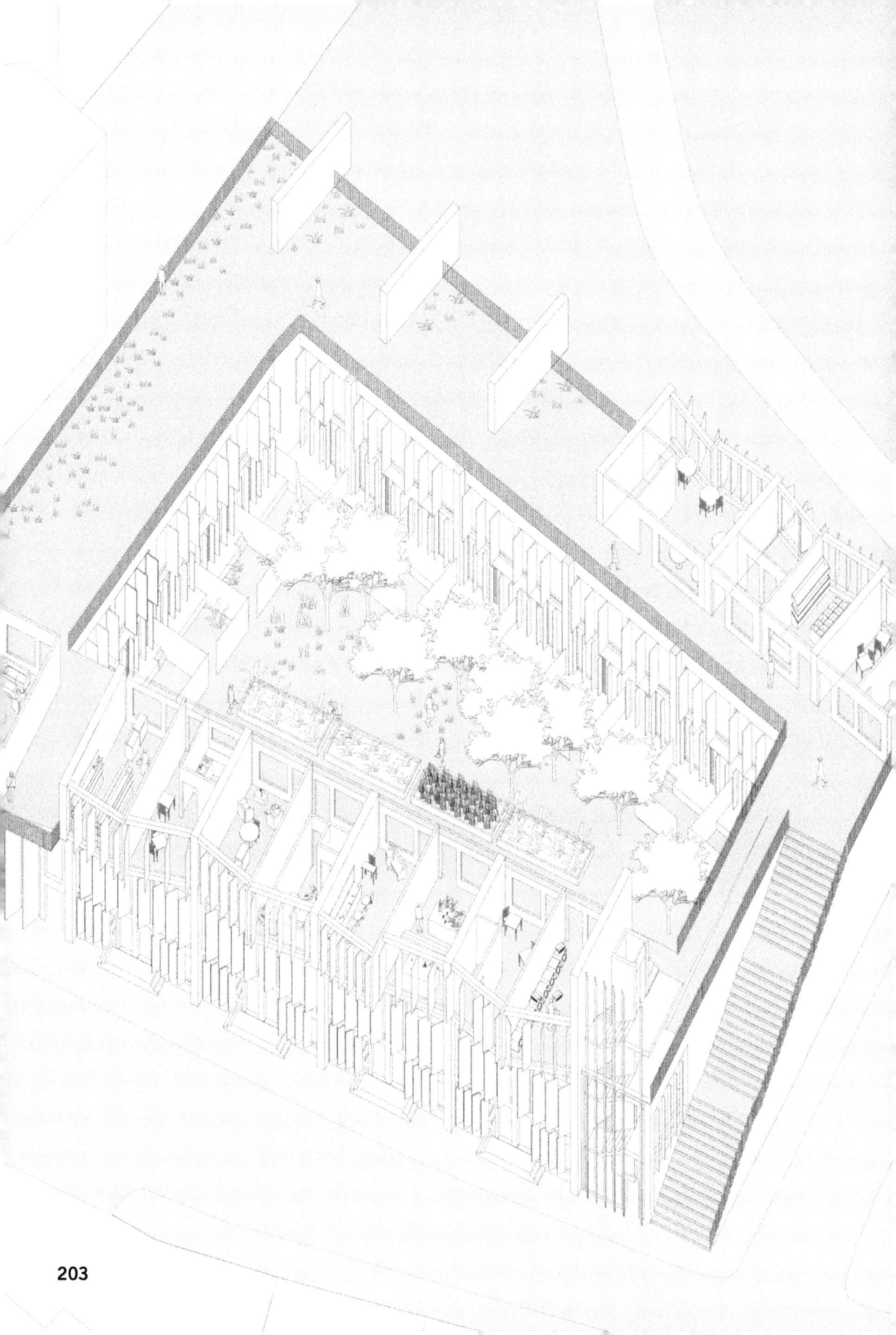

RE-HABITATION

JASMINE MONTINA

LOCATION: LONDON BRIDGE, LONDON, UK

This proposal asks what happens when the semi-communal/semi-private world of the outdoor space within a perimeter block is interrupted by public programmes and infrastructures.

Conceived as housing for post-operation patients in rehabilitation, the project is a perimeter block with 3 levels of duplex apartments on top of a therapy centre at the ground floor. The duplex apartments are arranged 3 to a cluster, where the entrances of the trio of homes open onto the same generous porch seating area, encouraging a sense of encounter and communal spirit. At the ground floor, the perimeter block is occupied by treatment rooms on two sides and a range of community spaces along the other two. This programmatic separation of the ground floor into the private and the public in turn divides the central external space into two, delineated by a colonnade that bisect the space. On one side of the colonnade, is a therapy garden for the use of the residents only. The other garden is accessible to the local community, and is flanked by community clinics, consultation rooms, and a large gym/hall space for hire.

This juxtaposition of the private and the public is further accentuated by a colonnaded public walk way that cuts through the community garden diagonally, connecting the street to the park. This allowed the proposal to become a piece of urban infrastructure and a part of the city.

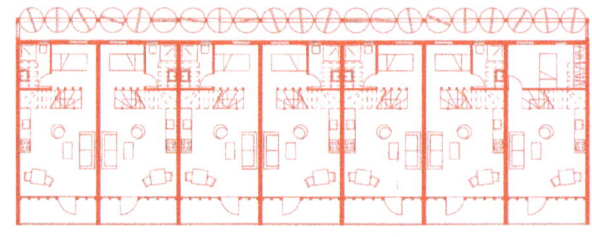

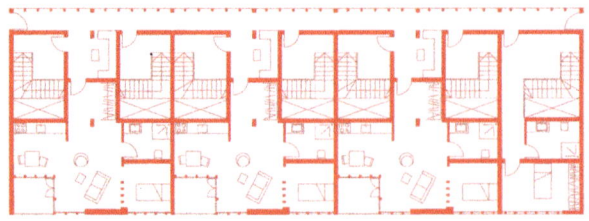

OPEN CAMPUS

GIA SAN TU

LOCATION: SOMERS TOWN, LONDON, UK

This project takes inspiration from the Oxbridge quadrants and cloisters but ask how this typically private and introvert typology can be hybridised with a wider public realm in a densely urban setting.

The project comprise a large number of student rooms arranged around two connected cloistered quadrants. On each floor above the ground, the student rooms are minimal spaces that open onto an accentuated and widened corridor, or a 'learning landscape.' Taking cues from examples such as the Cripps building and Harvey Court at Cambridge, these widened routes are flanked by deep benches, book shelves and desks looking over the quadrants, where students can come out of their room to spend time reading, studying, or socialise with each other. A secondary facade of moveable shutters turn these spaces into winter gardens when the weather gets cold, so they can continue to function.

On the ground floor, one of the two quadrants is dedicated to the students, being a scholar's garden surrounded by study, reading, and recital spaces. The other quadrant, however, is accessible to the wider community as a community park, with shops, cafes, laundrettes around it. The two quadrants are physically separated by a tall assembly and performance hall which narratively connects the two spaces together, as a place which is shared by both the students and the wider community.

HAPPY TOGETHER

BARBARA CELLARIO

LOCATION: NEW CROSS, LONDON, UK

This project takes inspiration from the courtyard housing typologies in Beijing and applies it to a co-housing enclave that seeks to re-establish a sense of urban intensity and communal life in a fragmented and under-served part of the city.

The proposal consists of three critical elements, a ground floor of communal and public facilities, a podium of residential outdoor spaces, and a collection of housing blocks that accommodate students and families.

On the ground floor, two courtyards, are enveloped by a series of communal spaces, including a swap shop, a creche, a library, a gallery, and a community hall. One of the courtyard is dedicated to the creche as a children's play space. This is where the proposal engages with the wider neighbourhood.

Above the ground level, the podium provides additional outdoor spaces, but only for the residents, from where they can look over the courtyard below. The housing blocks themselves are arranged based on the idea of co-living, where each block contains a series of flexible and adaptable shared spaces, be it an outdoor dining room or a loft games room. these moments of shared life are highlighted through the material palette, which uses a combination of standing seam copper cladding with charred timber, as well as glass bricks on the ground floor.

 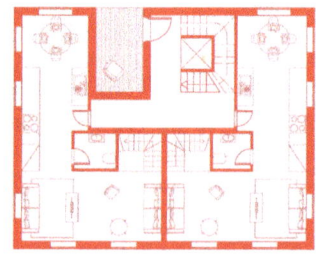 

PANORAMIC REFUGE

JACQUELINE ROSALES

LOCATION: NEW CROSS. LONDON, UK

This is a polemical project that challenges the mundane and the norm in social housing provisions. Conceived as a temporary housing project for those in urgent need of shelter, the project was inspired by interviews with potential tenants who wanted a place of distinctive identity that they could call home. This led to a fundamental rethink of how social housing can and should be places of spatial, material and aesthetic richness, even luxury.

Informed by this attitude, and inspired by the works of Zaha Hadid at Galaxy Soho in Beijing, Gaudi's Casa Mila, as well as the courtyards of Beijing, the project is a voluptuously curved building punctured by two generous courtyards/ lightwells. The form of the building allows for the creation of dual aspect duplex apartments with panoramic views across the local area and south London, with continuous blaconies that wrap around the entire facade, where neighbours can greet each other. Circulation is economised and occurs every other floor, accompanied by covered outdoor spaces the residents can make into their own. At the ground level, a library, a gallery, a nursery, a gym and a cafe connects the project with the wider neighbourhood. At the roof top, a greenhouse with panoramic views across the city is free to the public. The income from these none residential elements will offset the cost of the building and its maintenance in the long run.

COURTYARDS IN THE SKY

REMI KUFORIJI

LOCATION: FU GUO LI, BEIJING, CHINA

This project asks a simple question: if the perimeter block is seen as a vertical extrusion of the single storey courtyard, how can the qualities of the outdoor space at ground level be replicated at each level of a perimeter block?

Whereas the literal vertical extrusion of a courtyard plan inevitably creates a light well or atrium in place of any usable outdoor space, this project minimises the central atrium and instead carves out an open space along the perimeter edge of the plan. This tectonic move creates a large and deep outdoor space which is expressed on the facade as a double height recessed 'hanging courtyard'. This space is a temperate environment protected by a line of moveable glazing panels that can convert it from a 'hanging courtyard' into a winter garden over the cold months in Beijing. The height and depth of this space also brings more natural daylight deep into the plan, allowing the vertical circulation and the light well in the centre of the plan to benefit from the sun.

Around this space a range of 2 to 4 bedroom apartments for young couples and families are arranged over two floors. The activities in these 'hanging courtyards' are decided by the residents who have access to it, with a temporal element that allow it to change function as the seasons change, from outdoor dining room in the height of summer, to a greenhouse in the depth of winter.

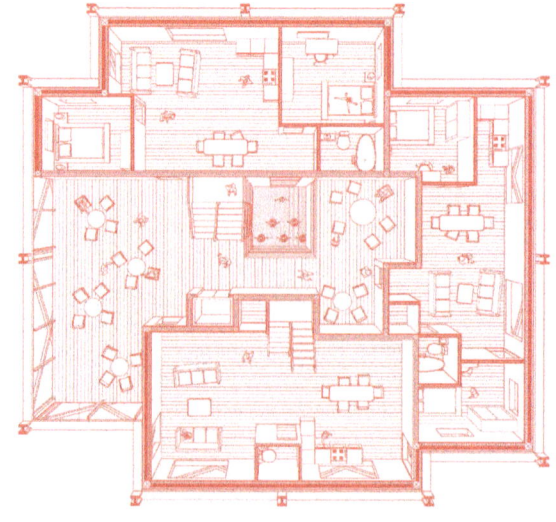

MEET YOUR NEIGHBOURS

REBECCA COOPER

LOCATION: HU JIA LOU, BEIJING, CHINA

This is a speculative and rhetorical project, which through its playfully manipulation of the perimeter block into a skyscraper, asks how seemingly disparate groups of people can dwell together.

Conceived as a response to the juxtaposition of gleaming office towers against dilapidating 1950s housing blocks in the Hu Jia Lou neighbourhood of Beijing, and inspired by Koolhaas's writing on skyscrapers as well as Torre David in Caracas, the project imagines a mutant building made of two halves, which seeks to create a dialogue between the white collar middle class office employees of the CBD and the blue collar migrant workers living in cramped conditions in basements in the nearby 1950s housing blocks.

The two halves of the building, paid for by the corporation occupying the top half, are tectonically slightly slipped against each other, with the top half clad in glass curtain wall and used as office spaces, and the bottom half as housing for migrant workers in expressed concrete and brick cladding, with flexible open spaces left throughout the plan for the inhabitants to take over and build over as their families grow and their economic position improves. The atrium allows daylight to penetrate into the building. Critically, it also allows for visual contact between the two disparate groups of occupants. The result is a phased project that evolves and changes its appearance over time, which both benefits from yet simultaneously satirises the power dynamics in capitalist society.

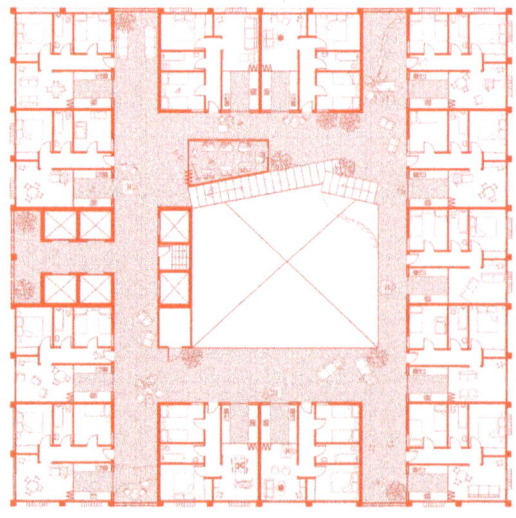

RESILIENT REFUGE

KRISTINA VELEVA

LOCATION: NEW CROSS, LONDON, UK

This housing project for families and vulnerable women combines the intimacies of the Beijing Hutongs and the clearly defined edges of the European urban block to provide a multi-tiered micro-townscape with a variety of communal spaces and a sophisticated transition in degrees of privacy.

At the ground level, the building is understood as a perimeter block, which contains a whole host of communal and public facilities. These range from shops, pottery studios, counselling services, a nursery and rentable community rooms. These programmes caters to the needs of the residents whilst connecting the building's occupants with the wider neighbourhood. Two small public squares are carved out from the massing of the block, in response to the well used church and a protected Eucalyptus tree, these are places to gather on a warm summer evening. Ascending from these open spaces, one arrives onto a raised podium on which clusters of two to three storey homes are carefully arranged. The tectonic complexity of this composition creates a hierarchy of different gaps between buildings, where families and vulnerable women in temporary accommodation are provided with outdoor spaces of different proportions and levels of intimacy, from generous play spaces to quiet breakout spaces. Within the buildings themselves, split level design ensures that occupants can see each other from multiple parts of the home, reinforcing a sense of safety and community.

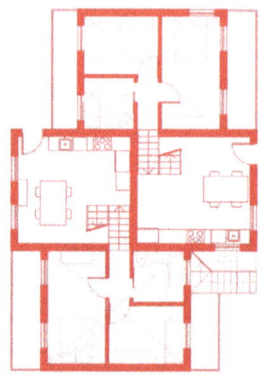 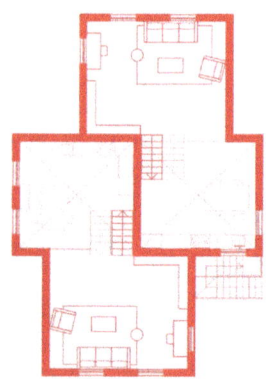 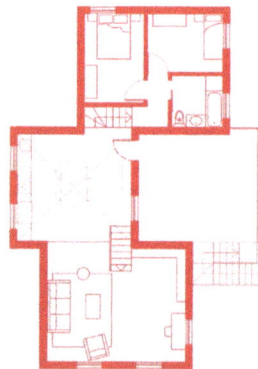

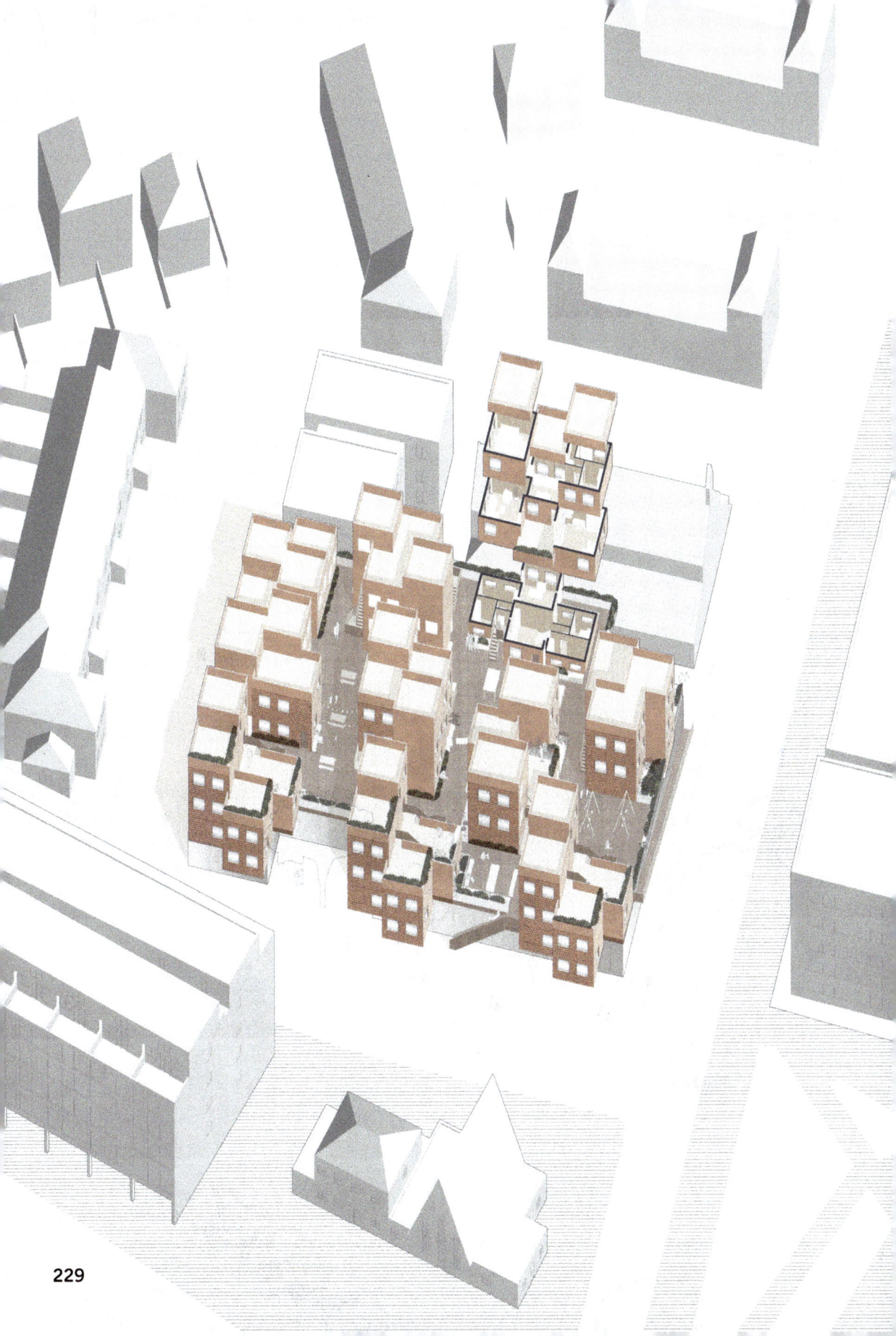

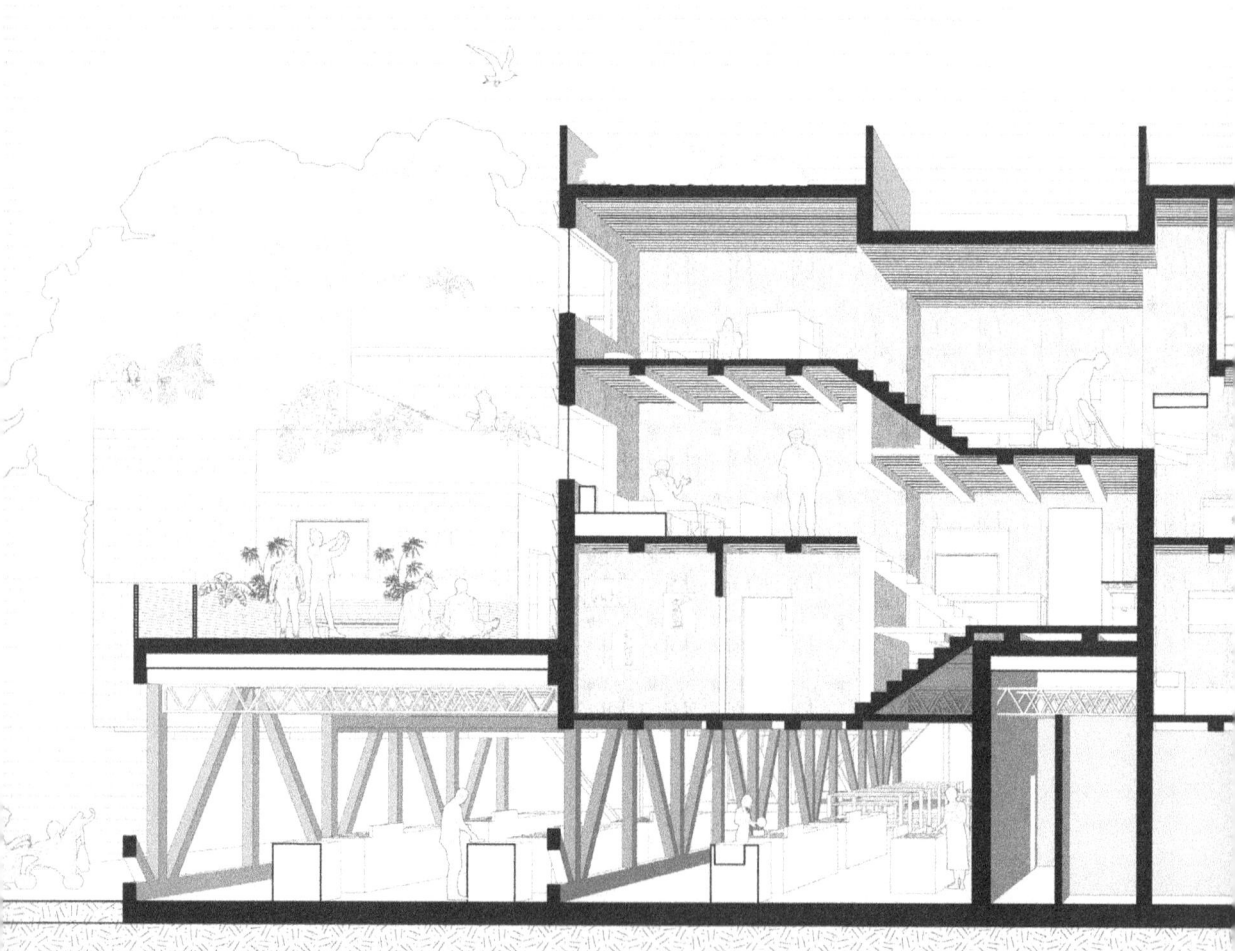

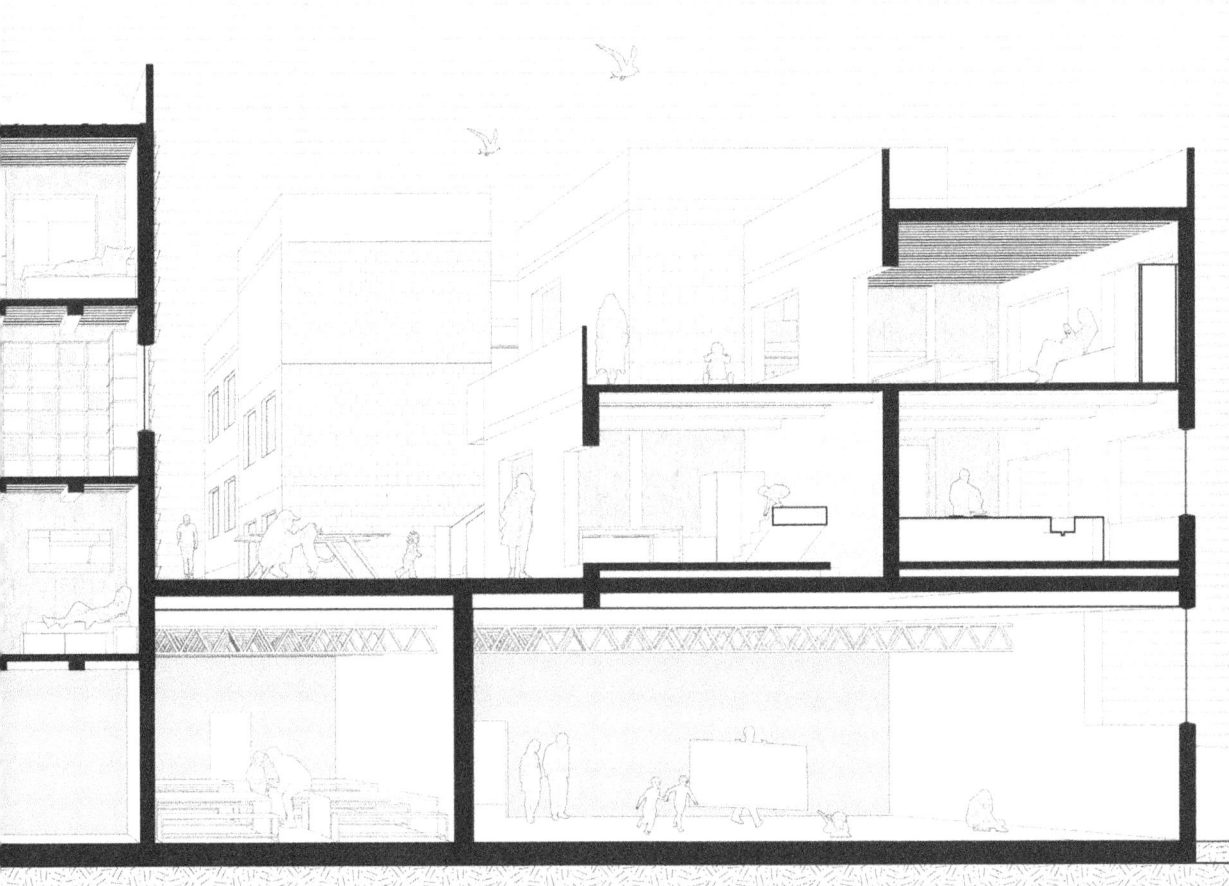

VARIATIONS ON A QUAD

BILLY NGUYEN

LOCATION: NEW CROSS, LONDON, UK

This project takes inspiration from both the Chinese courtyard and the Cambridge quad, and asks how a community can be curated around key moments of outdoor communal life.

The proposal take up the entire site, forming an urban perimeter block. However, instead of being inpenetrable to the city, the block is carved and punctuated to create five key outdoor spaces.

An allotment on the southwest corner opens onto the street corner through a gentle level change; a sunken sports court is visible from stepped seating created for passers by; a rector's yard and an ecological garden are both accessible from a newly created alley; a playground is visible through the building's cores but protected from the outside world. These outdoor quads are connected to each other through strategically located cores that are community rooms in themselves, linking up the indoor and outdoor common spaces of the project in one coherent journey.

The housing that sit over these outdoor spaces are based on a modular design system. All units are based on the same structural grid and adopt different tenure mix depending on the outdoor spaces that are adjacent to them, where family units over look the playground, couples units sit over the allotment, and student units envelope the sunken sports court.

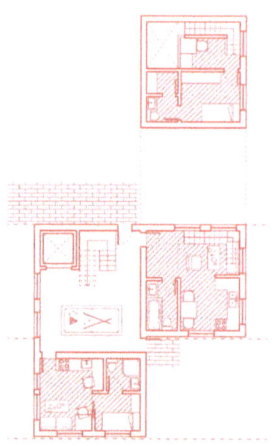
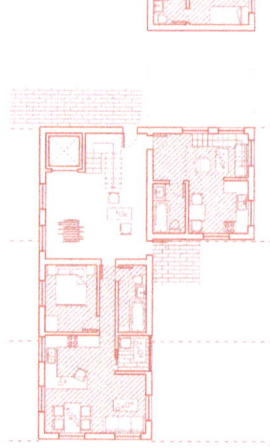
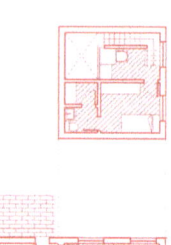

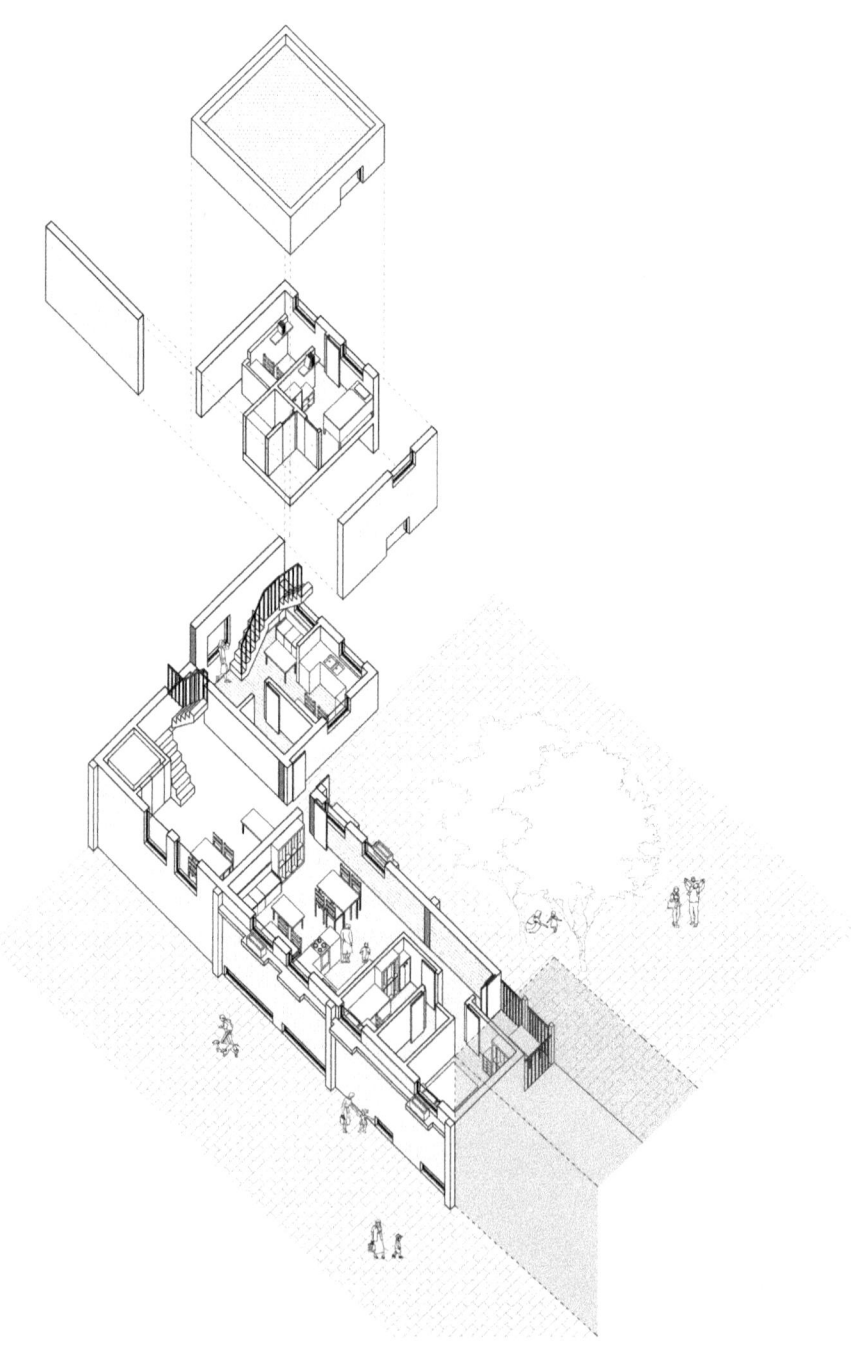

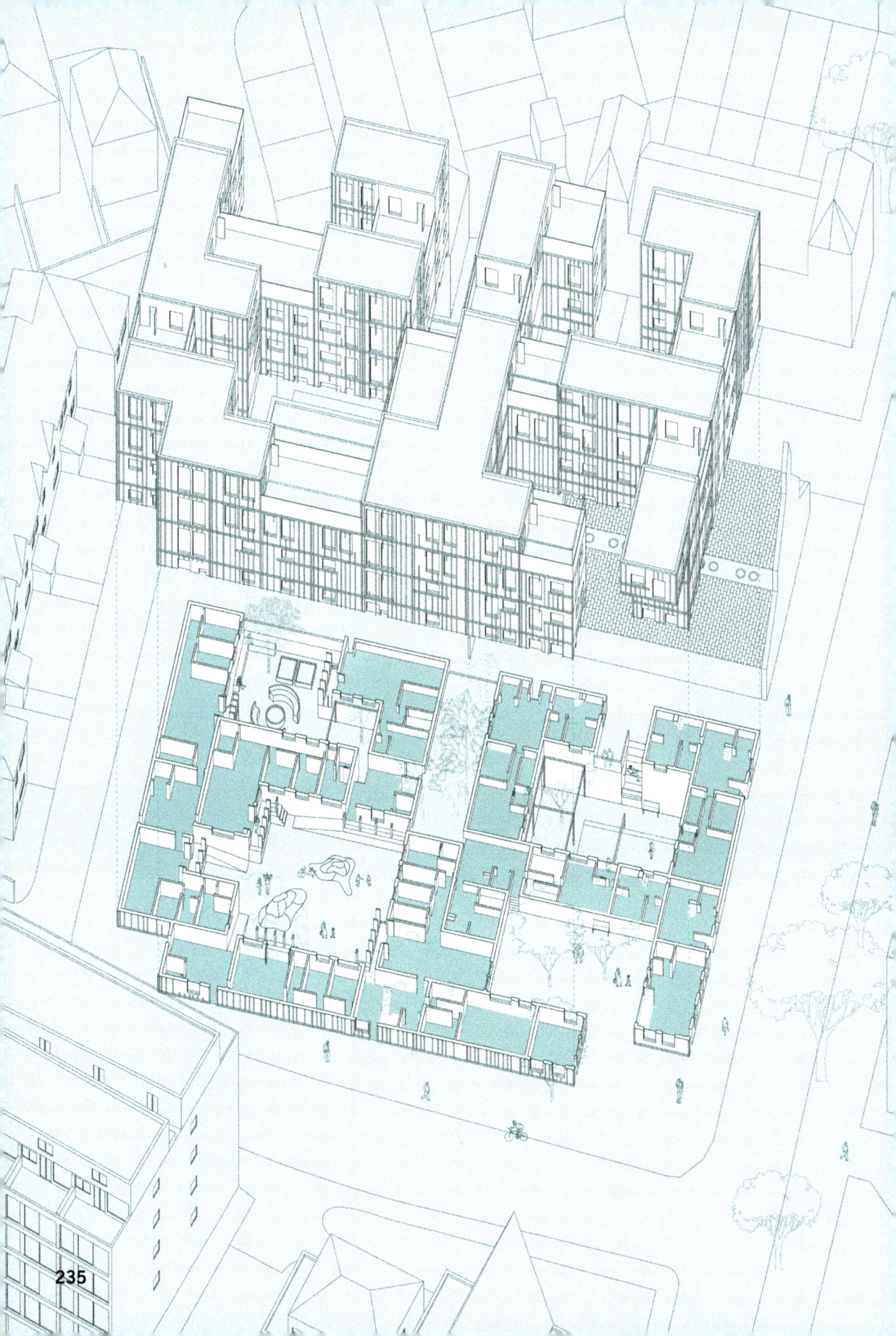

A NEW URBAN VILLAGE

RYAN SPEERS

LOCATION: SAN YUAN LI, BEIJING, CHINA

This project hybridises the perimeter block with the mat/courtyard typology to create a protective enclave that offers a complex, and rich world of interior and exterior spatial experiences.

Designed as a commentary on the prevalence of urban villages on the outskirts of growing cities such as Beijing, the project proposes to accommodate all of the low income migrants who works at this central Beijing market site. The proposal retains the existing market as well as the residential block occupied by local Beijingers.

Around these existing buildings, a perimeter is established that encircles the entirety of the site, within which a variety of terraced and courtyard housing typologies are deployed to further divide the proposal into a network of interconnected indoor and outdoor spaces.

The external courtyards vary in size, function, and levels of privacy. At the most basic level, they form small gardens shared by 2 to 3 households arranged around them. Slightly bigger outdoor spaces becomes more sociable gathering spaces, for the elderly ladies to perform their evening callisthenic dances or the families to sit amongst trees and catch the breeze.

Inspired by Liu Jiakun's Chengdu collective housing precedent, a running track utilising the rooftops of the entire proposal becomes a physical and metaphorical ribbon that bring the community together as a whole.

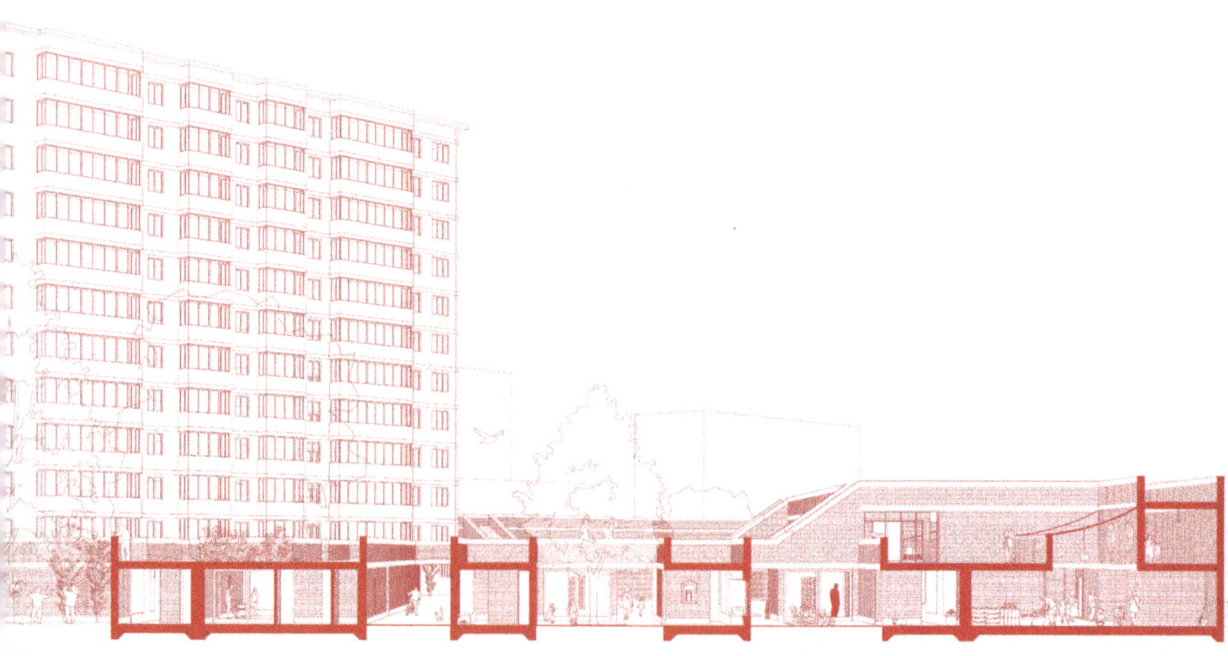

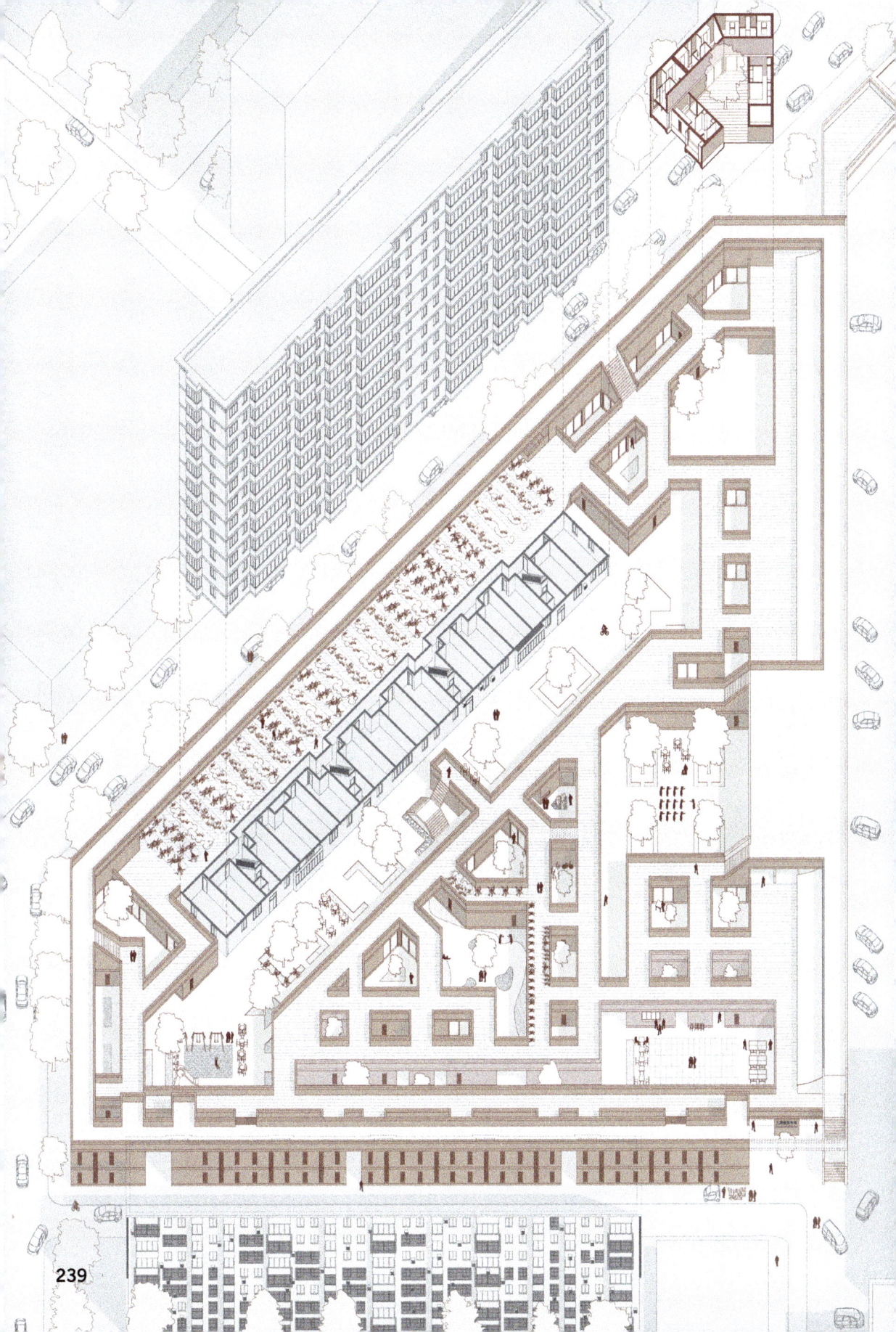

ON THE POETICS OF HABITAT

KEREN HE, DAVID PORTER, JOHN ZHANG

JZ: Ultimately, the studio asks students from China and the UK to dare to imagine new ways of living, or dwelling, in the city. The underlying optimism in the studio's agenda may be perceived as naive, but one might argue that it is precisely at this very moment in our shared global history, that optimism, idealism and dare one say, utopian vision, are in short supply. This collective endeavour was best summed up by Keren as the pursuit of 'the poetics of habitat'. Perhaps we could end the conversation by talking about our understanding of this term, from both Chinese and European perspectives, and somewhere in between?

KH: China today faces similar urban problems as it does in the West. The urban dwellings in Chinese cities are inexorably impacted by historical, political, social, religious, economical, geographical, and psychological factors, resulting in many unique characteristics over the years. The studio's briefs involve visualizing the city and housing of the future. From the beginning of the design process, students must ask a philosophical question: what is the ultimate concept of a human habitat? In traditional Chinese culture, it has always been understood that the "poetics of habitat" is the ultimate dream, not only for the literati, but for human beings in general. The classic 4th century poet Tao Yuanming wrote his well-known verse: "While picking asters 'neath the Eastern fence, my gaze upon the Southern mountain rests"(采菊东篱下，悠然见南山)[01]. The poem relates to the concept of *Yijing* (意境), an ideal which is also expressed in many other traditional art forms—poetry, painting, calligraphy, etc. Although the concept is more philosophic than practical, we believe for education it is important to keep an optimistic imagination for the future.

JZ: The writer who wrote the verses Keren quoted, Tao Yuanming, sought a hermetic life of solitude, having become disillusioned with public office and public life in the dying days of the Jin dynasty. For me, Tao's 'poetics of habitat' speaks of a life of aesthetic retreat into nature. Fast forward to the 21st Century, and things have become much more complicated. Most of us now live closely in densely populated urban or suburban locations, where housing shortage and housing insecurity are constant issues. Our homes are exchangeable commodities intimately tied into our global financial system, where we judge their value by looking at how much cash they are worth to its next owner. Looking beyond ourselves, humanity's impact on climate and the natural environment is so profound that a new geological epoch, the Anthropocene, has been declared. So what should be the 'poetics of habitat' for our time? I think it must begin with housing as a fundamental human right. We should be exploring new ways of living and sharing together, inviting intimacy from others, and provide an alternative to established property relations, which have distorted the idea of the home. We should be asking how dwellings can be made so as to leave our natural environment, which we do not possess, completely undisturbed.

These considerations remind me of Theodore Adorno's argument that we must learn 'how not to be at home in one's home' [02]. For me, beyond the original critique of property relations, this advice is also a useful starting point for us to re-consider our relationship to each other and nature in the act of dwelling.

DP: I would slightly re-phrasing your question, saying that for me, the studio was daring to imagine ways of dwelling at the meeting-point between new and old. I think it is evident that daily life is characteristically repetitive and routine, almost ritualised. It was interesting to visit Zaha Hadid's Galaxy and view people going about their lives. Someone is waiting for his girlfriend and fiddled with his cell phone to kill time. Thirty years ago, he would perhaps have simply smoked a cigarette to kill time. It is clear that these people have not been remade by the architecture, however extraordinary! Their mode for 'killing time' has been, however, technologically updated.

Keren started using the phrase 'the poetics of habitat' towards the end of our collaboration, and I really like it – it's a great summary of what we were trying to achieve. A concern and a sympathy for how people live their daily lives in the places we design for them. Daily life everywhere is an interaction between people and place where the inhabitants adapt to their habitat and they adapt their habitat to suit their changing needs.

The English architects Alison and Peter Smithson had a great phrase – 'the art of inhabitation' to describe how people adapt themselves and their environment on a day-to-day basis. As architects we design the habitat, so we set the game running, after that it is over to the inhabitants. Designing is our art, inhabitation is theirs.

Notes

(01) Tao Yuanming (365-427) *Drinking*. (transl. Yang Xianyi and Dai Naidie)
(02) Theodor Adorno, *Minima Moralia: Reflections From Damaged Life* (New York: Verso), 1974

A CONVERSATION OF RELEVANCE

JOHN EDWARDS

A CRITIC'S PERSPECTIVE

Reflecting upon the last few years of my role in the Joint International Design (JID) Studio, as a regular critic, it occurs to me that, irrespective of the specificity of its tectonic and formal investigations, the studio is primarily concerned with a strive for relevance.

At a fundamental level, the studio seeks for its output to be relevant to the simple reality of how people use space. David's observation of how people congregate around Zaha's building, and the timelessness and universality of this behaviour highlights the need to understand, at a fundamental level, how people occupy and move through a space, individually or in groups, wherever they are in the world.

Of course, a global relevance is the more obvious agenda. The studio makes it clear that a great deal of commonality exists in terms of the challenges and aspirations facing the inhabitants of both London and Beijing.

The exchange programme fosters a spirit of curiosity and open-mindedness, where it is incumbent upon the students to develop a nuanced and considered understanding of diverse global contexts in order to make useful contribution to the world in which we live – wherever that may be. Bringing together the distinct cultures of east and west elevates the discussion beyond local constraints and forces us to address matters of space as a human condition. In doing so the students are being prepared to leave with a mindset relevant to all corners of the world in which they wish to practice. This welcoming cross-fertilisation has facilitated the generation and representation of ideas that could not be born out of a single school, or indeed a single continent. Students are encouraged to develop their own critical position, refined through rigorous debate and investigation in both the UK and China, and the discussions that are triggered play an essential role in the ongoing vitality and pertinence of the studio. The very idea of a comparative programme exploring Chinese architecture in contrast to the Western agenda seems very timely for a de-colonialised curriculum.

In particular, it has been surprising to see how quickly CAFA Chinese students assimilate into the daily routines of university life in London. This has been helped, in part, by the diverse and multicultural student body at the

Discussing proposal with a student following a model workshop afternoon

University of Westminster, where students arrive from all over the world not simply to study the discipline but to immerse themselves in the rich and vibrant offerings of London's creative scene. Many of the CAFA students are in the UK for the first time, some having only recently begun presenting in English, but within a matter of weeks their confidence is revealed for all to see – and to critique. There is a visibly collaborative and welcoming environment among the group, evidently supported both here and in Beijing, which empowers students to express themselves.

The studio's decision to engage with housing design as a brief is also a highly relevant one. Housing is at once simple and incredibly complex, apolitical and yet loaded with political connotation. The complexity comes not from form-finding, but out of a rigorous exploration of the interplay between the personal and social, the private and the shared. Housing design offers an important lens through which to view the world: a learning device that often begins by revealing some sort of presumption or unconscious bias - forcing us to critically engage with our own living patterns - before offering clues as to how we may design for a safe and just place in which we all can thrive. The ambition is to create new forms of interaction and engagement that respond to a specific concern yet apply to a global outlook, which is no easy task. It takes courage to embrace this challenge and not rely on imaginary constructs to put forward solutions that could actually affect change.

By steering students toward low-rise high-density tectonics, the ambition is the exploration of ideas of an appropriate scale that sits between being so ubiquitous as to be acontextual, or so site-specific as to be unrepeatable, and thus largely irrelevant. This agenda necessarily situates itself in a rich cannon of post-war British modernist endeavours in a street-based urbanism, as well as a rich world of both contemporary and historic precedents in Beijing.

While the projects presented here describe a myriad of potential future poetics of habitation - distinguishable by typology, form, concept or material, these tectonic preoccupations appear to also be coupled with a drive for social relevance and sustainability.

In their work, the students have sought to address issues of care provision, homelessness, urban isolation, community-led development, the post-nuclear family unit, alongside the challenges of designing out waste, reducing carbon, increasing biodiversity and utilising modern methods of construction. The students are encouraged to develop new viable social scenarios and novel ownership models that take on the forces of capital and the market, that also challenge conventions of construction methods and materials, to produce projects that are better engaged with the realities of the world in which we operate, a conversation they must start having now as future practitioners in both Beijing and London, forewarned is forearmed.

The journey to successful outcomes is rarely smooth but can certainly be rewarding. Housing may not in itself solve a crisis, but people can. The studio's focus on housing allows graduates to be part of the conversation, engaging in the collaborative practices that we hope will affect beneficial change.

Engaging the everyday from a global perspective, the studio attempts to resist the trappings of transitory obsessions in aesthetics and 'theory'. There is a timeless quality to the work that this studio has produced which reinforces its validity. Overall there is a clear ambition to help students graduate as global citizens, who need not (and should not) all act the same but have the necessary skills to engage with a positive conversation anywhere in the world. Much of the success of this endeavour relies on conversation and building a shared understanding with others. I can't foresee a situation when this approach would not be helpful!

John Edwards *in an Architect and co-founder of e-gg, a small practice focused on de-carbonising the built environment. John studied at the University of Cambridge and the Royal College of Art. Alongside practice John teaches architecture to undergraduates at the University of Westminster and Canterbury School of Architecture.*

My tutorial with a CAFA student

AFTERTHOUGHT

JOHN ZHANG

NOSTALGIA, SENTIMENTALITY AND THE NEED TO TRAVEL

As we head into the next five years of our adventures at the Joint International Design (JID) Studio, this book has provided a much needed point of reflection for us to look back. The very act of putting the book together has sharpened our minds and brought to light a few realisations about our critical positions, approaches, processes, and output, which now bears clarifying as a series of 'afterthoughts'.

Overwhelmingly, there is a detectable sense of nostalgia when it comes to the ideas of living together in the city.

In the UK, there is a renewed interest in the works of Neave Brown and his contemporaries, such as Benson & Forsyth, Evans & Shalev, Peter Tabori, etc. The high density, low rise, street based urbanism of this generation of architects mostly working as local authority architects, is now the focus of much scholarly research output and professional veneration, inspiring a new generation of architects, academics, and students in their own pursuit of the 'poetics of habitat'.

In China, architects such as Wang Shu have long lamented the demise of architectural culture in the city, going as far at times to deem the city beyond saving. For Wang Shu, the poetics of habitat is to be uncovered from the spatial, material, and narrative logic of the Literati world view from China's past, specifically how architecture mediates between man and nature. In this sense, Wang Shu's work can be said to be nostalgically transgressive, against the general current of banal and rapid development in China.

In both China and the West, issues of housing shortages, demographic shifts, and changing patterns of co-habitation has also revitalised an interest in past models of shared or communal living, which for China, remains a recent memory. The Fusuijin apartment building, with its minimal family homes and communally shared kitchen and dining spaces, still looms over its Siheyuan neighbours, a constant reminder of days of collectivisation. This Chinese precedent can trace its lineage to buildings like the Narkomfin building in Moscow, an example of the idea of the Social Condenser espoused by the Soviet Constructivist. In fact, there is a renewed fascination with the works of Marxist spatial and cultural theorists from the 1960s within the certain youthful quarters of Chinese architectural academia and profession, where the works of Adorno, Tafuri and P. V. Aureli are enjoying a re-reading after four decades of Socialism with Chinese Characteristics.

The corridor from a socialist era collectivised housing block, where residents have taken over the space with personal belongings

Indeed, Aureli's critique of the family dwelling as a space fundamental to capitalist production, and his idea for the complete strip down of private spaces in order to engender a radically new paradigm for shared living, is finding great resonance globally, in places like London as well as Beijing, where architects are looking for solutions to tackle increasing housing shortage and un-affordability.

Looking to the past to inform the future is an essential and critical practice in architecture. However, the rose-tinted glasses of time have the tendency to turn reflective criticality to pleasant remembrance, which distorts historicity, and at its worst, turn us into unwitting participants in processes which then exploits this nostalgia.

For example, one is always reminded that despite subsequent western fascinations with the Social Condensers, collectivised models of living in China and the Soviet Union were, at their core, an effort to subsume family relationships and a private life under the individual's relationship with the collective, or the state. The proliferation of makeshift private kitchen stalls in the dark corridors of collective housing projects like Noarkomfin and Fusuijin are a evidence of the residents' resistance to the encroachment of their private life in the model of collective living being promoted under this particular spatial ideology. Ironically, P.V. Aureli's calls for a radical reinvention of the idea of housing through experimentations in collective property in resistance of capitalism, have since become co-opted by capitalism into new forms of private real estate. In co-living and co-working developments like The Collective and WeWork in London, a higher profit margin is extracted from the inhabitants by persuading them to pay more for less personal space under a sentimental narrative of the 'collective' (a collective of consumers as far as the developer is concerned), and the interior is designed to evoke a sense of nostalgia of some sort of authenticity as to the identity of the physical space and its inhabitants.

In the case of Wang Shu, one might question whether the detectable nostalgia in his work is capable of more than just a form of resistance and transgression. Whilst the traditional relationship between dwelling and landscape are undoubtedly both poetic and aspirational, there are clear problems of scalability when one applies this approach to the reality of contemporary urbanity in China. Wang Shu's Qianjiang Shidai high rise housing project in Hangzhou, his first and last one, and a source of frequent frustration, is a constant reminder of the challenge facing this nostalgic view of dwelling when it has confronts issues of density, economy, and the market. Wang's next housing project

Qianjiang Shidai, Hangzhou, Wang Shu's only high rise housing project

On the road: students outside the Rockbund Art Museum in Shanghai

was a boutique rural regeneration project of a handful of dwellings under the auspice of municipal patronage: the complete opposite of Qianjiang Shidai in every way.

As far as the radical tectonics of Neave Brown's generation is concerned, it is critical to understand that these built realities were facilitated by and contingent on the political will of a few very specific organisations and individuals. Camden Council in the late 1960s with Sydney Cook as the head of its architecture department were pivotal in the realisation of many of the exceptional housing projects we hold so dear today in London. However, the political climate that was conducive to so much creativity was very short-lived, and was pushed aside by the onset of Thatcherism in the 1970s. Today the number of council housing has fallen to their lowest level since record began, a meagre amount of affordable housing is being produced each year, as we continue to deal with a crisis of housing shortage and homelessness. So the relevant question now is not whether a high density low rise urbanism can work in our cities today (we know it can), but what kind of political, social, cultural and professional agency we must create as architects to facilitate and support these novel tectonics.

This question of agency is central to our future as architects, and it lies in our ability to not only imagine new spaces, but also new relationships and new processes. In this sense, it has never been more vital to look globally. China and the UK can inform each other, the mistakes we each make are cautionary tales for the other, the successes we each enjoy set precedent for the other to follow. The Chinese writer Lin Yutang said that 'a good traveller is one who does not know where he is going to, and a perfect traveller does not know where he came from.' This brings us back to our agency as a studio, to encourage travel, to foster a global conversation, and to open up new perspectives, so we might tear down boundaries, at a time when the world seems busy putting them up, and imagine how we could dwell poetically together.

LEARNING FROM BEIJING

A VISUAL ESSAY BY STAFF AND STUDENTS OF THE JID STUDIO

ACKNOWLEDGEMENTS

First and foremost, I would like to thank Professor Lindsay Bremner for her invaluable advice and support throughout the making of this book.

I am also extremely grateful to Professor Harry Charrington, whose wholehearted and ongoing support has been critical in the growth of our studio and the development of our bespoke pedagogical approach.

This studio would not exist without Professor David Porter, who, in his dual role as visiting professors at Westminster and CAFA, has been pivotal in the conception of the exchange programme between our two institutions. The studio has benefited from his intellectual generosity, and a lifetime's knowledge as a practitioner, academic, and educator.

I would also like to express my gratitude to Professor He Keren, who has played a critical part in the development of our joint programme over the last 5 years, and contributed significantly to this book. Her warmth and expertise have made the UK students feel right at home, away from home.

We are also very grateful to the tutors who have contributed significantly to the teaching of the studio: John Edwards in London; Liu Siyong, Hou Xiaolei, Han Tao, and Wang Zigeng in Beijing.

Our thanks also go to Professor David Dernie, and Professor Lü Pinjing, who, in their respective roles as the former Dean of the Faculty of Architecture and Built Environment at the University of Westminster and the former Dean of the School of Architecture at CAFA, were instrumental in initiating contact between the two institutions, which eventually led to our programme.

Our thanks also goes to Douglas Murphy, for not only contributing to this book, but for being a regular critic for the studio, whose knowledge and insights continue to benefit the studio. Our gratitude also goes to other regular critics who have joined us over the years, including Fergus Feilden, Quinn Greer, Natasha Reid, Sarah Beth Reily, and Edward Simpson.

We are also extremely grateful to the Education Section of the Chinese Embassy in the UK, for supporting our students in obtaining scholarships from the China Scholarship Council. Specifically, we would like to thank the Minister Counsellor for Education, Mr Wang Yongli, as well as Ms Ruan Shao and Mr Li Xiaopeng for their personal support over the years.

The making of this book would not have been possible without the help of Signe Pelne, a former student from our studio. Thank you for your tireless work in bringing the content together and contributing to the writing.

Most importantly, I would like to thank all the students of the Joint International (JID) Studio over the years. Your work, some of which are featured in this book, have been a critical part of the studio's inquiry into housing design in different contexts, as well as the development of a comparative pedagogy that could nurture these endeavours. Your willingness to try something new and your adventurousness is the lifeblood of the studio.

Past members of the Joint International Design Studio:

2015-16
Rebecca Cooper, Amrit Flora, Maria Garvey, Max Pahlberg, William Rowe, Caroline Wisby, Gao Pengfei, Liu Zishen, Liu Mingxi, Liu Minpei, Lyu Jiayi, Miao Jiuying, Sun Yuchang

2016-17
Irina Bodrova, Jasmine Montina, Bryan Ortiz, Zuza Osiecka, Heenah Pokun, Hugo Shackleton, Anissa Souza, Karol Wozniak, Shi Zeyuan, Zuo Dan

2017-18
Aris Apatsidis-Jones, Anderson Barbosa Sales, Rebecca Foxwell, Gabija Gumbeleviciute, Dilan Kalayci, Remi Kuforiji, Signe Pelne, Drew Yates, Chen Zhaoming, Qin Jiachen, Tong Yujia, Xie Yufan, Zeng Wentao, Zhang Yuqin

2018-19
Poonam Ale, Lauren Fashokun, Manjot Jabbal, Maheer Khan, Matthew Lindsay, Ryan Myers, Ryan Speer, Yana Stoyanova, Catalina Stroe, Gia San Tu, Soraia Viriato, Gao Wenhui, Huang Jiamin, Lai Chin In, Lyu Lyu, Tong Zixiao, Zhuo Zishun, Zou Jialiang

2019-20
Lucy Bambury, Barbara Cellario, Rujina Chaudhury, Billy Nguyen, Jason Prescod, Jacqueline Rosales, Anna Tabacu, Kristina Veleva

A Tale of Two Cities

Joint International Design Studio 2015-2020
Edited by John Zhang

A University of Westminster, School of Architecture and Cities Publication

Designed by Mark Boyce

All texts ©2020 the authors

This work is subject to copyright. All rights are reserved, whether the whole or part of the material is concerned, specifically the rights of translation, reprinting, re-use of illustrations, recitation, broadcasting, reproduction on micro films or in other ways, and storage in databases. For any kind of use, permission of the copyright owner must be obtained.

ISBN 978-0-9929657-7-8

The Studio as Book series are available to purchase at www.studioasbook.com

The editors have attempted to acknowledge all sources of images used and apologise for any errors or omissions.

School of Architecture and Cities
University of Westminster
35 Marylebone Road
London
NW1 5LS

www.ingramcontent.com/pod-product-compliance
Lightning Source LLC
Chambersburg PA
CBHW041237240426
43661CB00067B/2908